STOP!

D0454122

You are going the *wrong way!*

Manga is a *completely* different type of reading experience.

To start at the *BEGINNING*, go to the *END!*

That's right! Authentic manga is read the traditional Japanese way-from right to left, exactly the opposite of how American books are read. It's easy to follow: just go to the other end of the book, and read each page-and each panel-from the right side to the left side, starting at the top right. Now you're experiencing manga as it was meant to be.

Attack on Titan: Before the Fall volume 7 is a work of fiction. Names, characters, places, and incidents are the products of the author's imagination or are used fictitiously. Any resemblance to actual events, locales, or persons, living or dead, is entirely coincidental.

A Kodansha Comics Trade Paperback Original
Attack on Titan: Before the Fall volume 7 copyright © 2015 Hajime Isayama/Ryo Suzukaze/Satoshi Shiki
English translation copyright © 2016 Hajime Isayama/Ryo Suzukaze/Satoshi Shiki

All rights reserved.

Published in the United States by Kodansha Comics, an imprint of Kodansha USA Publishing, LLC, New York.

Publication rights for this English edition arranged through Kodansha Ltd, Tokyo.

First published in Japan in 2015 by Kodansha Ltd., Tokyo as *Shingeki no kyojin Before the fall*, volume 7.

ISBN 978-1-63236-225-4

Character designs by Thores Shibamoto
Original cover design by Takashi Shimoyama (Red Rooster)

Printed in the United States of America.

www.kodanshacomics.com

9 8 7 6 5 4 3 2 1
Translation: Stephen Paul
Lettering: Steve Wands
Editing: Haruko Hashimoto
Kodansha Comics edition cover design by Phil Balsman

KODANSHA COMICS
DEVIL SURVIVOR
AFTER DEMONS BREAK THROUGH INTO THE HUMAN WORLD, TOKYO MUST BE QUARANTINED. WITHOUT POWER AND STUCK IN A SUPERNATURAL WARZONE, 17-YEAR-OLD KAZUYA HAS ONLY ONE HOPE: HE MUST USE THE "COMP," A DEVICE CREATED BY HIS COUSIN NAOYA CAPABLE OF SUMMONING AND SUBDUING DEMONS, TO DEFEAT THE INVADERS AND TAKE BACK THE CITY.
BASED ON THE POPULAR VIDEO GAME FRANCHISE BY ATLUS!
© Satoru Matsuba/Kodansha, Ltd. All rights reserved.

INUYASHIKI

A superhero like none you've ever seen, from the creator of "Gantz"!

ICHIRO INUYASHIKI IS DOWN ON HIS LUCK. HE LOOKS MUCH OLDER THAN HIS 58 YEARS, HIS CHILDREN DESPISE HIM, AND HIS WIFE THINKS HE'S A USELESS COWARD. SO WHEN HE'S DIAGNOSED WITH STOMACH CANCER AND GIVEN THREE MONTHS TO LIVE, IT SEEMS THE ONLY ONE WHO'LL MISS HIM IS HIS DOG.

THEN A BLINDING LIGHT FILLS THE SKY, AND THE OLD MAN IS KILLED... ONLY TO WAKE UP LATER IN A BODY HE ALMOST RECOGNIZES AS HIS OWN. CAN IT BE THAT ICHIRO INUYASHIKI IS NO LONGER HUMAN?

COMES IN EXTRA-LARGE EDITIONS WITH COLOR PAGES!

Inuyashiki © Hiroya Oku/ Kodansha Ltd. All rights reserved.

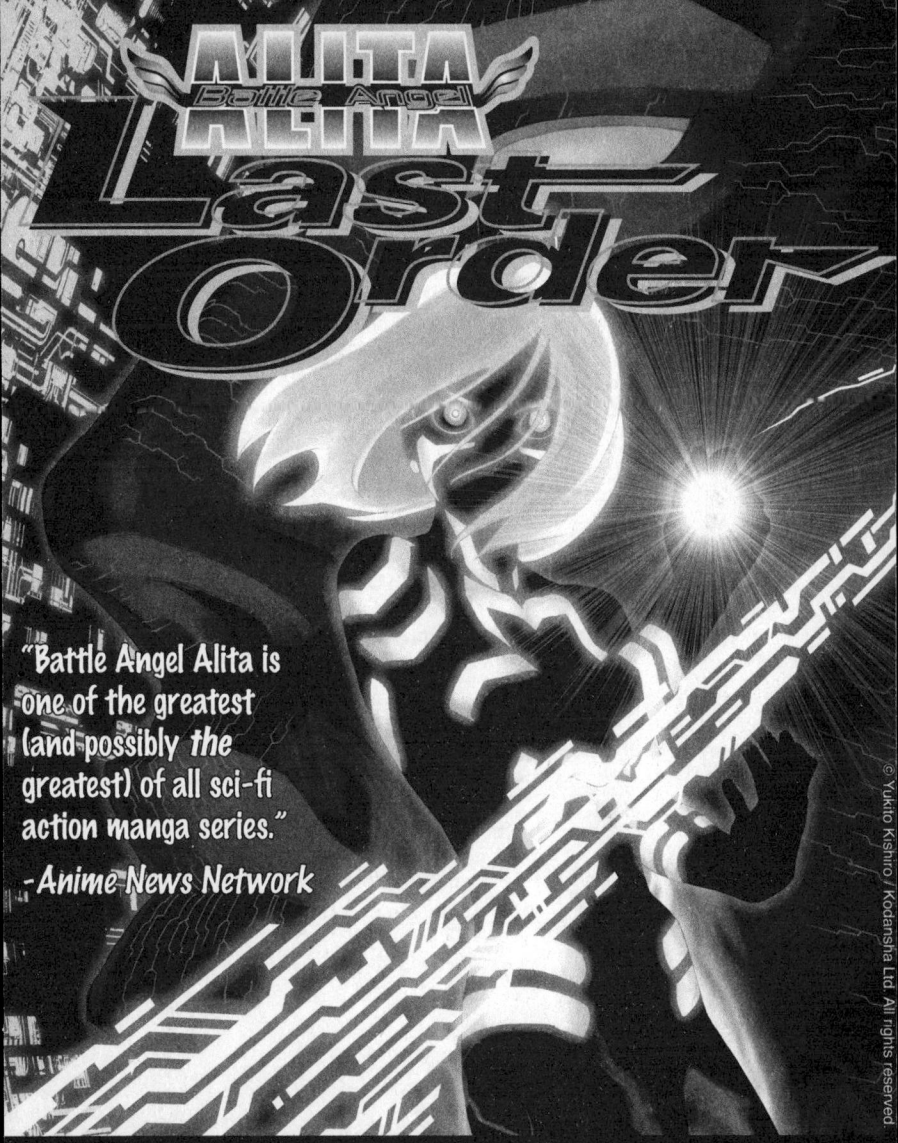

The Cyberpunk Legend is Back!

In deluxe omnibus editions of 600+ pages, including ALL-NEW original stories by Alita creator Yukito Kishiro!

KC KODANSHA COMICS

SAVE THE DATE!
Celebrating 15 Years
FREE COMIC BOOK DAY
1st SATURDAY IN MAY!
May 7, 2016
www.freecomicbookday.com
FREE COMICS FOR EVERYONE!
Details @ www.freecomicbookday.com
/freecomicbook
@freecomicbook
@freecomicbookday

Swear Upon Wall Maria · End

...TO REFUTE THE IDEA THAT WE CANNOT KILL TITANS!
THAT'S THE ONLY POSSIBLE WAY...
...I CAN REPAY HIM FOR WHAT HE DID FOR ME!!

I JOINED THE GARRISON CORPS TO PROTECT OUR HOME FOR SORUM TO COME BACK TO...
...AND NOW, I'M PROUD TO DO MY JOB.
I'M STAYING.
WHO
MARIA... WHAT WILL YOU DO ABOUT THE CORPS?
SORUM'S ALREADY-
AND YOU, ANGEL... WHAT WILL YOU DO NOW?
I...
I MUST DEVELOP A NEW WEAPON...
I NEED TO GO BEYOND THE WALL AGAIN!

I'M SORRY, MARIA...
SNORRR
IN ORDER TO SAVE MY LIFE...
...HE GAVE HIS OWN...
I'M CERTAIN !!!
I'M CERTAIN...IT WAS A HEROIC END, RIGHT ...?
...YES...
BUT... HE WAS A DAMNED FOOL!

FOR THE SAKE OF MARIA AND THE BABY SHE'S CARRYING...
...!!
NEXT TIME...
HRMF
IT STILL DOESN'T FEEL REAL.
...IT'LL BE MY TURN...TO PROTECT THE HOME...
ROLL
...FOR MARIA, THE BABY...AND EVERYONE ELSE TO LIVE WITHOUT FEAR...

...YOU SAID YOU'D PROTECT MY HOME SO I COULD RETURN...
AND ANGEL... YOU'VE BECOME A CRAFTSMAN TO MAKE THE WEAPONS TO DEFEAT THE TITANS...
WHEN I SAID... I WANTED TO JOIN THE SURVEY CORPS...AND SEE OUTSIDE THE WALL...
I'M FILLED WITH GRATITUDE !!
...ANGEL...
HOW-EVER...
TRANS-FER?!
THE NEXT EXPEDITION... IS GOING TO BE MY LAST. I'M GOING TO TRANSFER OUT OF THE SURVEY CORPS.

SIGH...
ゴクMRMM
PLUS, I ALREADY GOT AUTHORIZATION FROM CAPTAIN JORGE.
I CAN'T BELIEVE THIS!
TWO OF MY OLDEST FRIENDS, GOING BEYOND THE WALL TOGETHER...
BUT-!
WHAM!
I'M GRATEFUL THAT YOU KEPT OUR CHILDHOOD PROMISE...
SORUM! YOU'VE HAD TOO MUCH.
...MARIA!!
WE'RE GRATEFUL TO YOU FOR PROTECTING A PLACE GUYS LIKE US COULD COME HOME TO...

MURMUR
MURMUR
BUT THAT'S NOT A GOOD REASON... IT'S TOO DANGEROUS FOR AN AMATEUR TO BE THERE!
MURMUR MURMUR
YES. I WANT TO SEE IF THE CAPTURE NET I'M DEVELOPING WILL REALLY WORK ON THE TITANS.
NO. I NEED TO SEE IT IN ACTION WITH MY OWN EYES.
STILL, THERE'S NO NEED FOR YOU TO GO OUTSIDE THE WALLS, ANGEL!
IT'S ALL RIGHT!! I'LL KEEP ANGEL SAFE!

...HE WAS OUT THERE...
WAS SORUM...
...HEROIC?
IS IT TRUE THAT YOU'RE JOINING THE EXPEDITION, ANGEL?!

WHEN IT HAPPENED...
...I WAS WAITING HERE FOR EVERYONE TO RETURN FROM THE EXPEDITION.
...I SEE...
...
I REMEMBER GETTING THAT SINKING FEELING IN MY GUT WHEN I SAW THE BLACK SIGNAL.
JUST A WEEK AGO...

HAHH...
HUFF...
GRK
WHOOSH

ATTACK on TITAN
BEFORE THE FALL
Swear Upon Wall Maria

クリ
HNG

SWEAR UPON WALL MARIA

A story about the relationship between three childhood friends—Sorum Humé, who perished against Mammon in the flashback of Volume 6; his fiancée Maria Carlstead, a member of the Garrison Corps; and the genius craftsman Angel Aaltonen, future developer of the Device.

Originally published: Bessatsu Shonen Magazine, September 2015 issue

ATTACK on TITAN
BEFORE THE FALL

TO BE CONTINUED

THIS PRACTICAL TEST HAS SHOWN ME WHAT IMPROVEMENTS IT NEEDS.
AND THIS IS WHAT WILL MAKE THAT POSSIBLE.
TODAY MADE ME CERTAIN OF THAT.
NEXT TIME... I WILL DEFEAT OGRE !!

I AM GRATEFUL TO MY MOTHER AND FATHER FOR GIVING BIRTH TO ME.
BUT... MY ONLY FAMILY IS SHARLE.
IT WAS THROUGH MEETING SHARLE THAT I UNDERSTOOD THE EMOTION OF HAPPINESS.
I CAN FIGHT, NOT FOR VENGEANCE, BUT FOR THE SAKE OF MY LIVING FAMILY AND THOSE I HAVE MET...
I FIGHT THE TITANS—NOT FOR THE SAKE OF THE PAST, BUT FOR THE SAKE OF TOMORROW!

I...
I SUPPOSE THAT AS A SON... I SHOULD SWEAR VENGEANCE FOR MY FATHER AND MOTHER...
BUT... I CANNOT FIGHT FOR PEOPLE I'VE NEVER MET.
ESPECIALLY...
...WHEN I'VE NEVER CONSIDERED MYSELF TO BE UNFORTUNATE...

WHEN HEATH'S HEAD GOT THROWN BACK OVER THE WALL, AND ELENA SAW IT...
...WELL, YOUR MOTHER'S MIND SIMPLY SNAPPED.
...SHARLE ...?
MISS SHARLE TOLD ME ABOUT IT.
AND NOT ONLY THAT, KUKLO. THAT TITAN RUINED YOUR LIFE.

...!!
AT THE TIME, HEATH WAS A SUBORDINATE OF MINE...
HE WAS BOLD, DARING...AND A DAMN FINE SOLDIER.
OGRE BROUGHT ALL THAT TO AN END...
...AND HIS WIFE ELENA WAS CLOSE TO CHILD-BIRTH...
OF MY ENTRANCE CLASS, HE WAS THE FIRST TO MAKE SQUAD LEADER...

THAT TITAN, "OGRE"...
...YEARS AGO, THE SURVEY CORPS NICKNAMED THAT INDIVIDUAL TITAN "OGRE."
OGRE ?!
HE WAS DOWN THERE ?!
WE RAN ACROSS HIM ON THAT EXPEDITION, BUT THANKS TO YOU, MANY LIVES WERE SPARED.
OH... REALLY ...?
HEATH MANSEL...
YOUR FATHER WAS ONE OF HIS VICTIMS.

I ALWAYS KNEW...
...I WOULD HAVE TO TELL YOU SOMEDAY...
...FROM THE MOMENT I LEARNED THAT YOU WERE THE "TITAN'S SON"...

THAT BASTARD ...
...YEAH...
...THAT TEN-METER BASTARD WAS HERE THE WHOLE TIME...

YOU WERE THE ONE WHO SAVED MY LIFE.
I'M THE ONE WHO SHOULD BE THANKING YOU.
THANK YOU... YOU CAME BACK TO SAVE ME...
ARE YOU KID-DING ...?!
CARDINA TOLD US WHAT HAD HAPPENED, AND CARLO DECIDED TO GO DOWN WITH HIM.
CARDINA NEVER HESITATED ABOUT GOING BACK FOR YOU.
YOU CAN TALK LATER! WE NEED TO TEND TO HIM FIRST!
WE'LL LOWER KUKLO IN THE GONDOLA MEANT FOR WALL MAINTE-NANCE.
I... SEE...
THANK YOU... CARLO.
SOMEONE FROM OUR SQUAD WILL GET IT SET UP.
JUST HANG ON!

CAR-DINA...
I DARESAY YOU'VE GOT FRACTURES ALL OVER.
IT'S NOT JUST A BROKEN ARM. YOU'RE COVERED IN BRUISES...

GREEEEEE
GREE
AGAIN...
I FAILED TO DEFEAT THEM...

C... CARLO...
TO THINK...
...THAT I WOULD RUN ACROSS THIS ONE AGAIN HERE...
VMM!

THWAM
HUH?
RGH...
AH...!!
GGHK
OUCH ...
C...
CARDINA...

!
VOOM
KSHUNK
UH...
OH!
GSH
I'LL CRASH INTO THE WALL!!
RGH...
IT'S NO GOOD! I CAN'T STABILIZE MY POSITION!

PSHOO
DMM
GREEE
THERE! AT LEAST THE HORIZONTAL WIRE STILL WORKS!
IF I CAN HOIST THIS ONE...
DMM

GAH!
AH!
VOOM
BWOOSH
HRGH...
MMF!!

THE VERTICAL HOIST ISN'T WORKING?!
IS IT...BECAUSE OF THAT LAST SHOCK...?

WHAP
THUD
GNF
G-GOTTA PULL IN... THE WIRE...
GHK...
RRGK...
GAAH...!
WHAM
AH...

AAA
AA
HRNG
A
A
AA!
THWAM
AA...
AGGH...

ZMMF
THE FIVE-METER TITAN...
I SEE... IT SMACKED ME AWAY...
MY RIGHT... ARM...!!
ZIP

BAAM
WHAT...THE...?

DRSH
YES!!
NOW JUST SHIFT TO THE NECK...
SHUD

ZMMM
SHIT!!
BUT I'M NOT DONE YET...
HRG
I CAN STILL AIM FOR THE NECK!!

KUKLOOOO!!

DAMN!! HE JUST JUMPED AS I WAS GOING TO REACH HIS NECK!!

KUKLO!!!
TUG
!
BECAUSE OF KUKLO'S SIGNAL A MOMENT AGO...
THEY'RE PULLING ME UP!!

...AND GO!!
BOOM
DOOM
WAIT, IS THAT...?

BA-BUMP
ALL OF ITS ATTENTION IS ON CARDINA NOW...
BEFORE IT CAN BRACE ITSELF TO JUMP AGAIN...
BA-BUMP
...I WILL END THIS !!!
BA-BUMP
FOCUS ON THE TITAN'S NECK...ON THE ANGLE...
RATTLE
CALM DOWN...
RATTLE

BA-
BUMP

...THIS IS MY CHANCE...TO AIM STRAIGHT FOR THE BASE OF THAT TITAN'S NECK!!
BA-BUMP
BA-BUMP

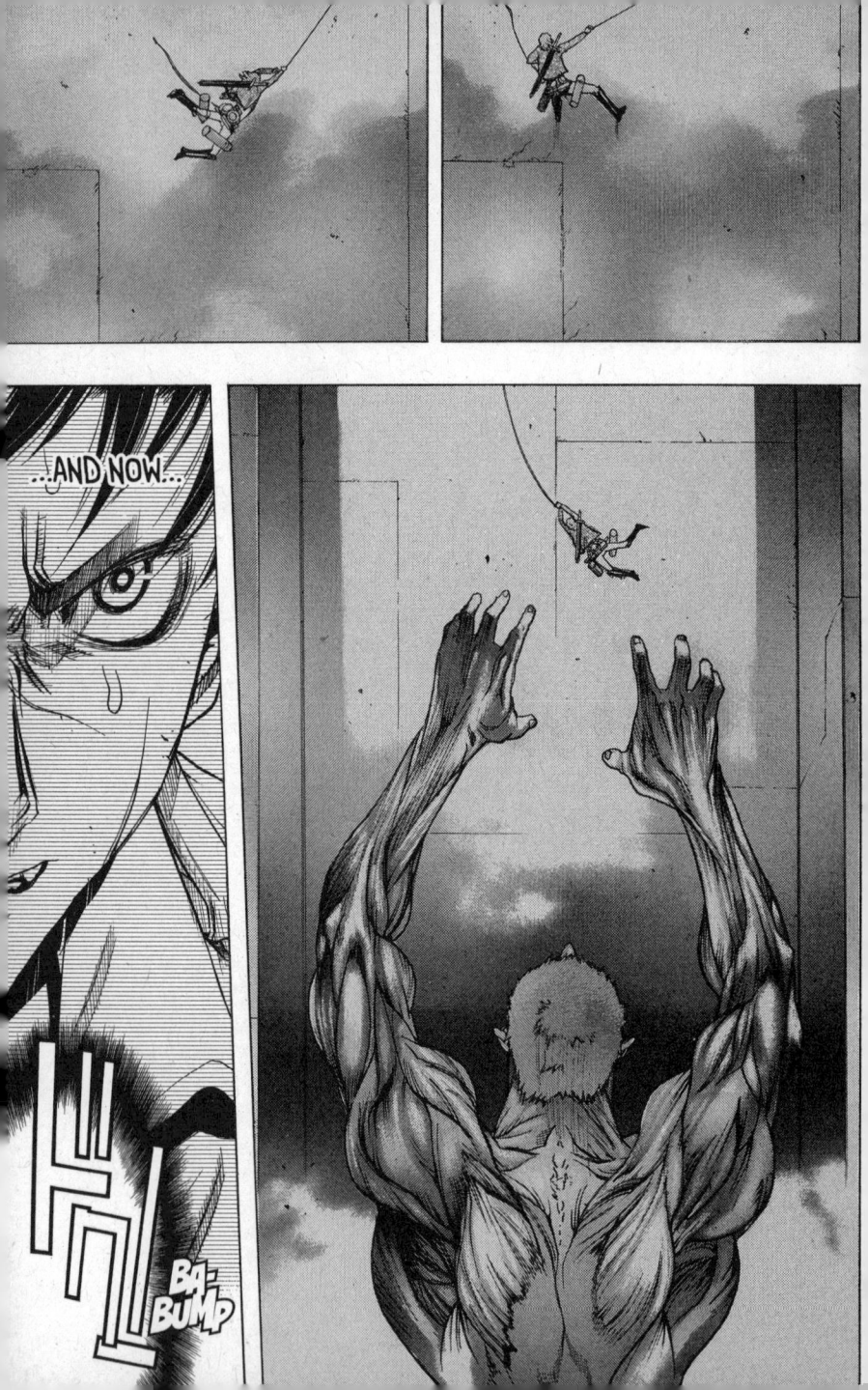
...AND NOW...
BA-BUMP

THAT SIGNAL MUST HAVE MADE IT UP TO THE TOP OF THE WALL.
THAT SHOULD SAVE CARDINA, AT LEAST!!

GRE
TE TE
TE E

THE EMERGENCY HAUL-UP SIGN!!!
DOWN THERE!
WHAT ?!
DAD !!
RIGHT !!
GRRRRRRRE...E
GRP

...SAY...
IS THAT KUKLO ?!
DID YOU...HEAR A VOICE?
AH!!
DID IT SOUND LIKE KUKLO SAYING, "NO!" TO YOU?
...YES.
IT WAS HARD TO MAKE OUT THROUGH ALL THE WIND...

!!
SPARKS!!

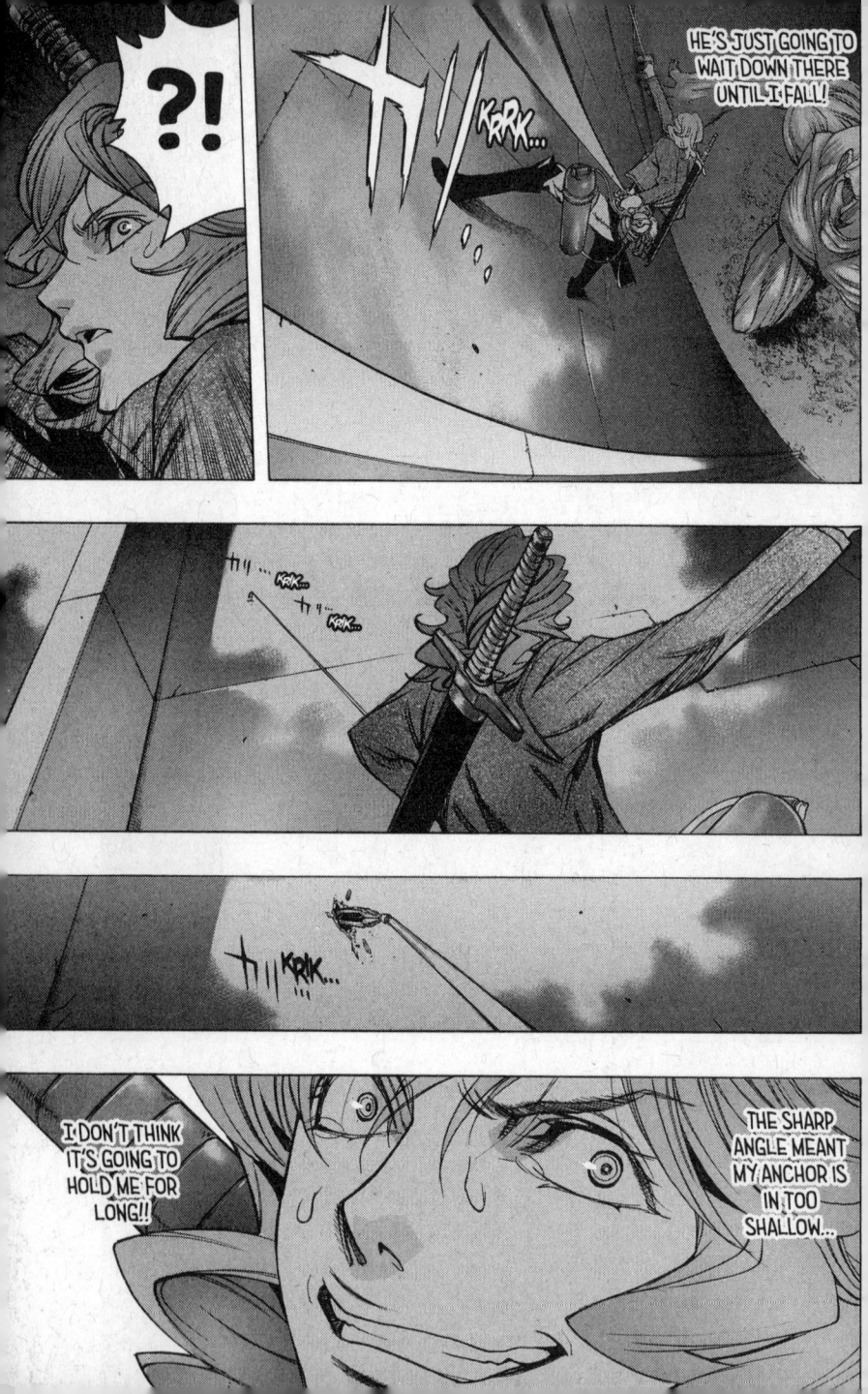
?!
HE'S JUST GOING TO WAIT DOWN THERE UNTIL I FALL!
KRRK...
KRIK...
KRIK...
KRIK...
THE SHARP ANGLE MEANT MY ANCHOR IS IN TOO SHALLOW...
I DON'T THINK IT'S GOING TO HOLD ME FOR LONG!!

LOOK AT THE SIZE OF IT!!!
SO THIS...IS WHAT THE INFAMOUS TEN-METER TITAN LOOKS LIKE...
SHIVER
OH CRAP, OH CRAP, OH CRAP!!!
KCHING
KCHING

KRIK
PHEWWW!
I SURVIVED ...I GUESS ?!
GULP

HE USED THE DEVICE TO ESCAPE !!
CURSE!!

ZOUMM
TO THINK THE WEIGHT OF THE NEW DEVICE WOULD COME INTO PLAY NOW, OF ALL TIMES...
IF ONLY...I'D REALIZED CARDINA WAS HERE EARLIER...
URGH...
?!!
CARDINA...

CHOMP
...!

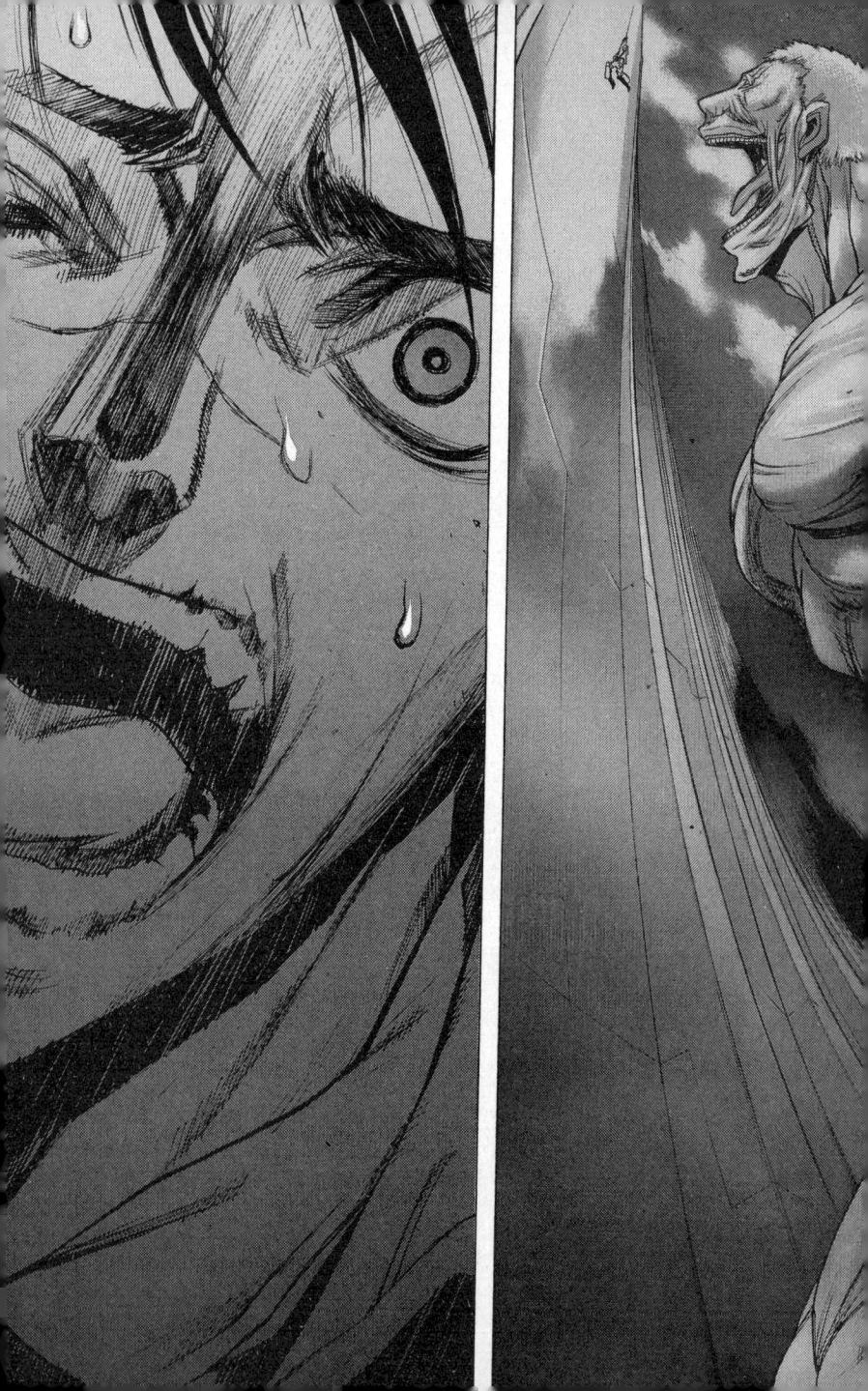

Chapter 24: Wail from the Shadows

MY BODY FEELS...SO HEAVY...
ONLY NOW DO I FEEL THE WEIGHT OF THE DEVICE...

ATTACK ON TITAN

BEFORE THE FALL

Chapter 23: Rondo of Darkness · End

NO...
Noooo!!
DSHH

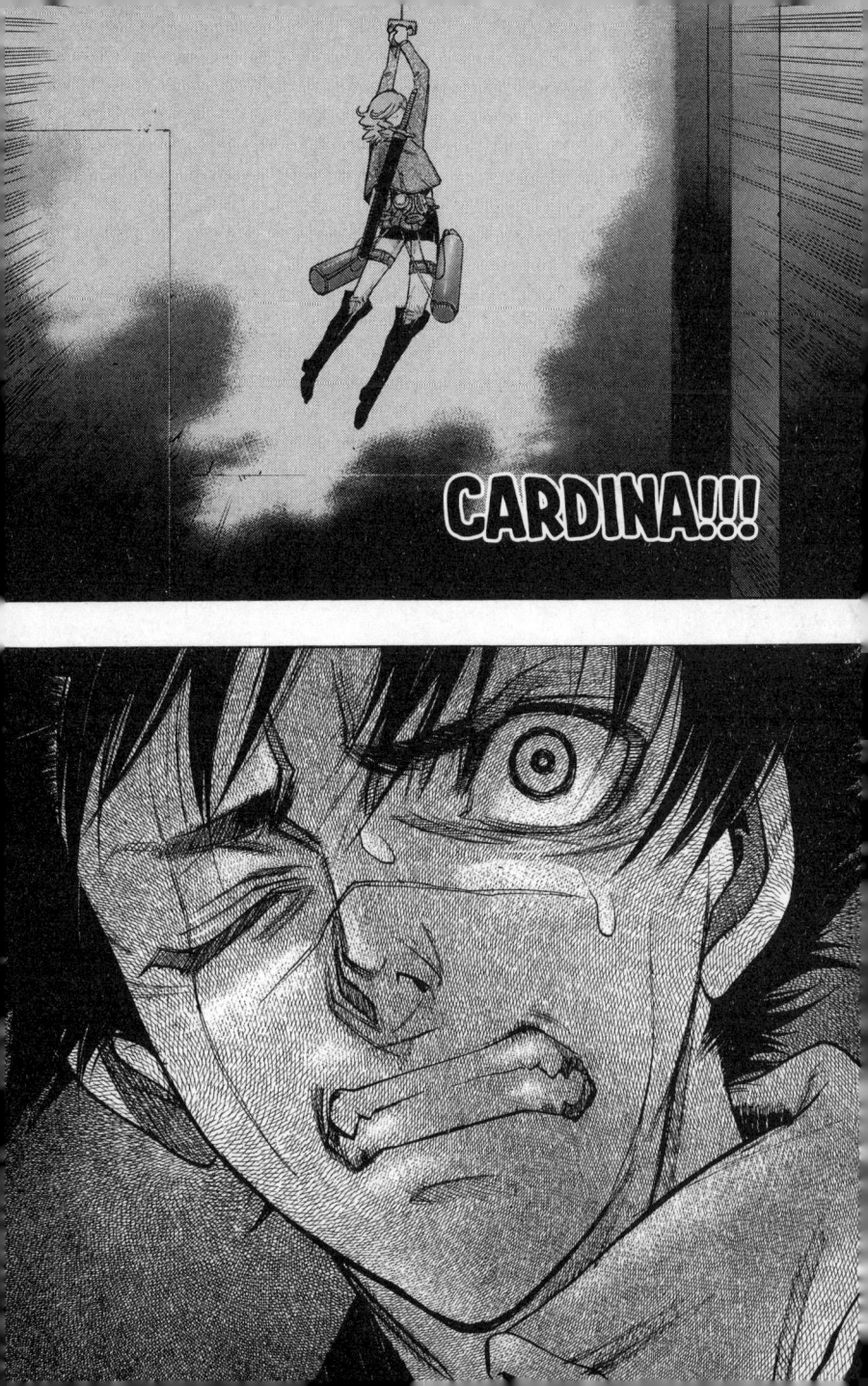
CARDINA!!!

...WHA ...?!
ZRD
BOOM
HNNG!
BWOOSH

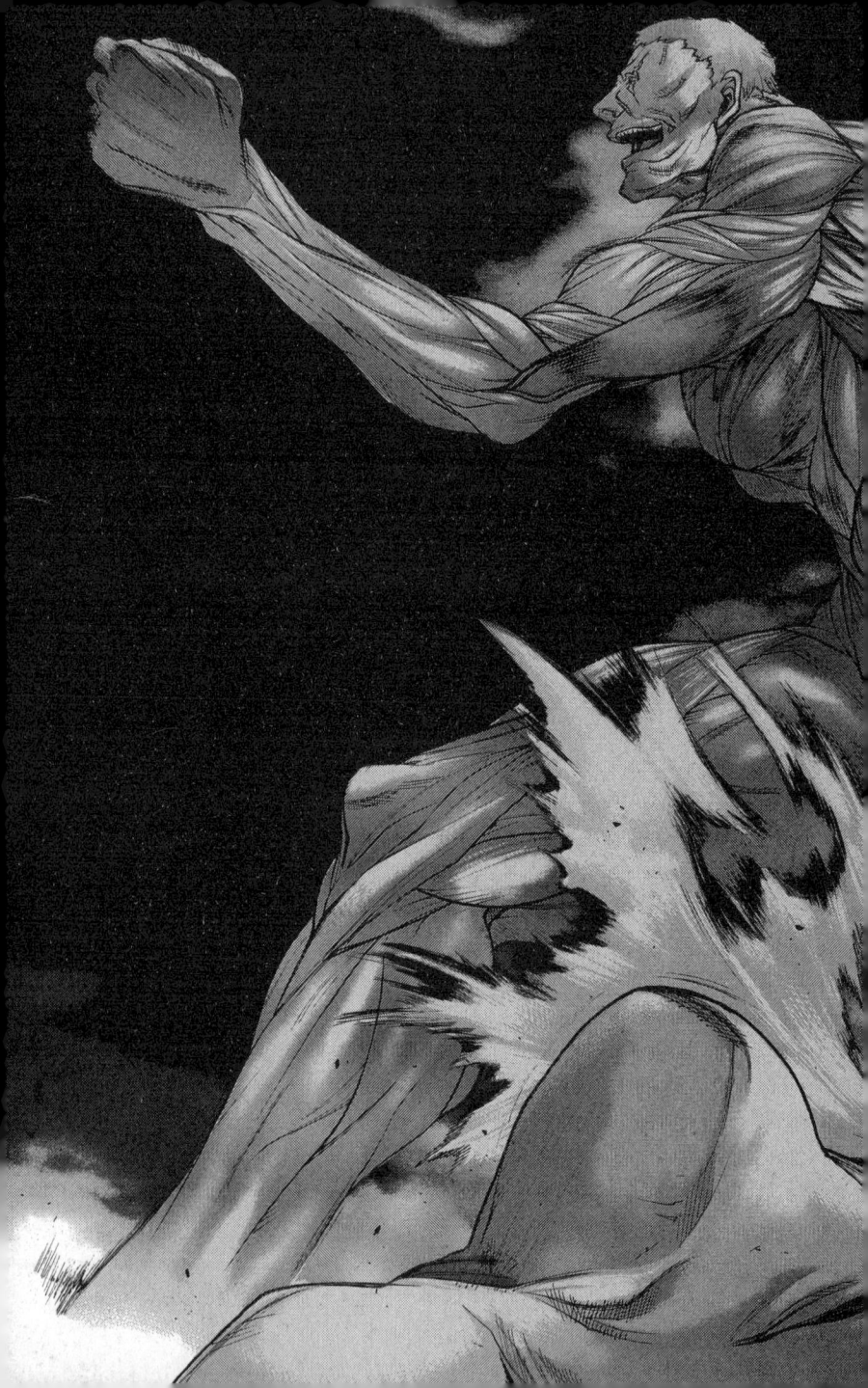

CALM DOWN...
BA-BUMP
STAY COOL...
FFFFH...
FFFFH...
BA-BUMP
IT MIGHT HAVE SNIFFED ME OUT, BUT IT HASN'T SPOTTED ME YET...
BA-BUMP
REMEMBER YOUR TRAINING !!!
BA-BUMP
STRIKE FIRST !!
...AND THEY GET BACK ON THEIR FEET!
BEFORE THE FIVE AND THREE-METER TITANS' ANKLES HEAL...

WHUD
WHUD
...IT'S ALL RIGHT.
WHUD
RATTLE
B-BUMP
B-BUMP
RATTLE

WHUD
WHUD
HOW FAR CAN THEY SENSE MY SCENT?!
HMPH
RGH!
THERE WERE ONLY TWO OF THEM WITHIN 500 METERS JUST A MINUTE AGO!

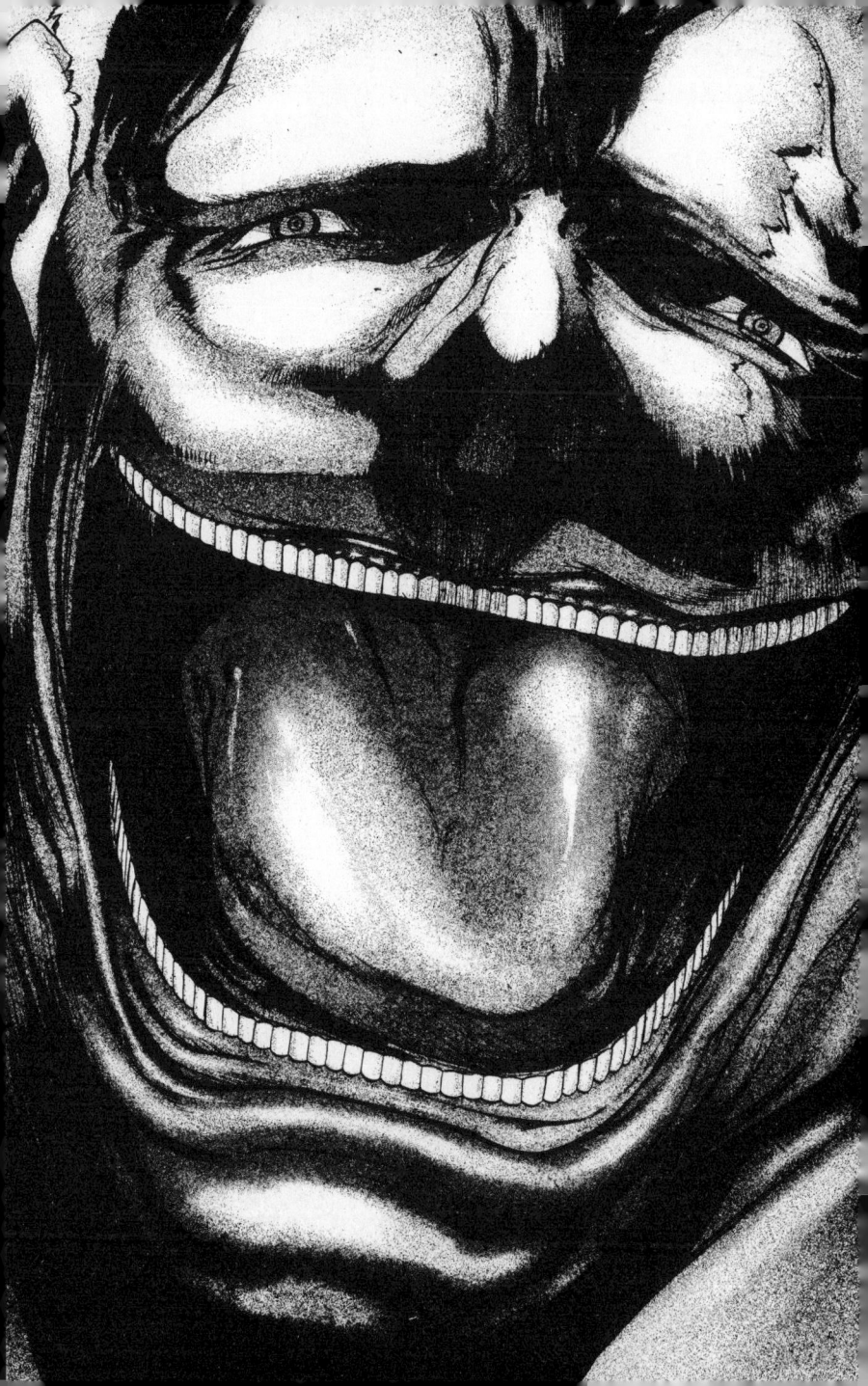

ANOTHER ONE!!!
BA-BUMP

DMM

THUMP
THWOP
FLOP
FSSHHH

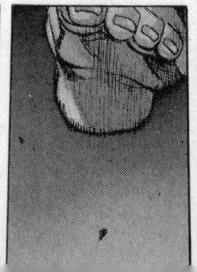

BOOM
ドボー
SLICE
BSHT

SPLATCH
SLUMP
WRCH
ZR
RK

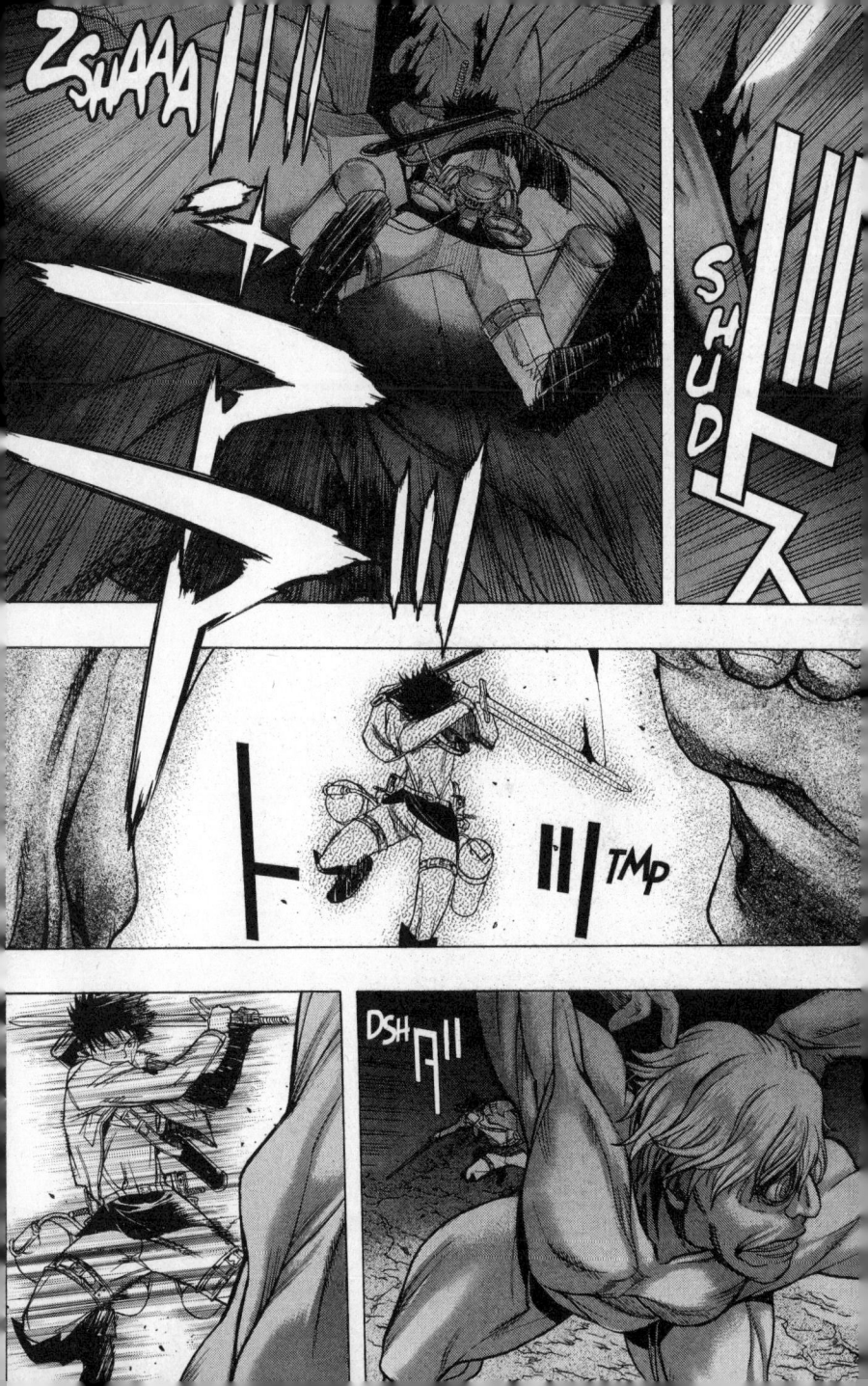
SHUD
TMP
DSH

!!
DMM
...NO GOOD...
ZRRP

ZNSH
GO DEEPER !!
SHIT...
CAN'T KEEP... BALANCE!!
I CAN'T GET ENOUGH LEVERAGE TO SINK THE SWORD!
WHOA...
FLOP
FLOP
ZRP
ZZRP

BWAA
THIS IS THE SPOT!

GRK
GREEEE

LOSING...
CONSCIOUSNESS...
...AND SMACK
AGAINST THE
GROUND...
IF I
FALL...

!!
WHAM
I'M IN... TROUBLE...
URBL...
IT ALREADY REGREW...ITS ARM...

I CAN DO THIS!

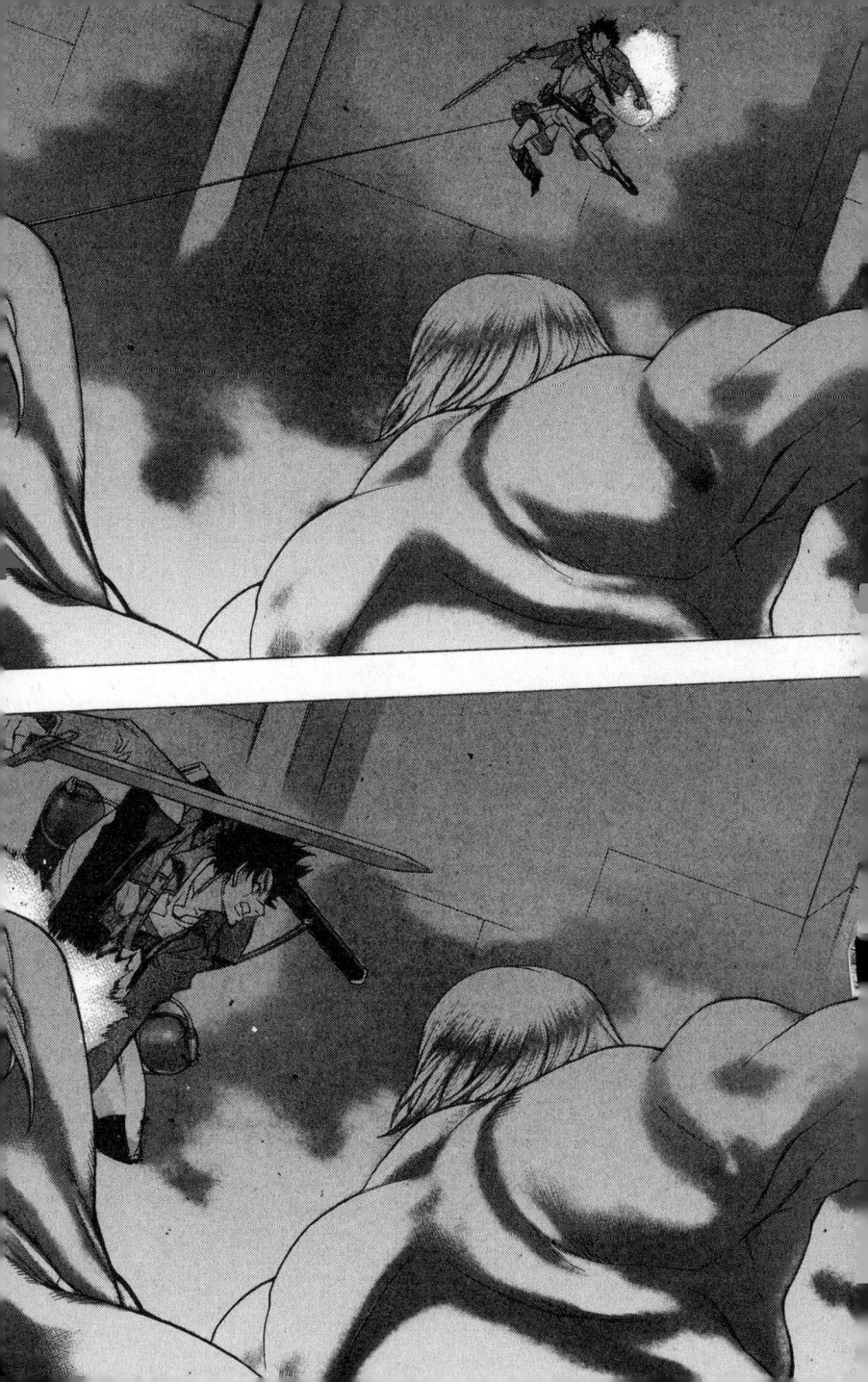

BWAK
PSHOO
BOOM
HRGH!
GREEEE
GREEEE

THUMP
CRAKK
ASHUNK
GREEEE

BSHOOM
GAK
GLURK
GNNG
GREEEE
BOOM

RAAH !!
VOOM
PAK PAK
YANK

...YOU!
BOOM
GOTCHA!
BSHOOM
RGH...
IT'S REGENERATING!!

KCHAK
BSHOOM
GREEE
THERE! NOW IF I PULL OUT THE ANCHOR...
BLSHT
NEXT UP IS...

MWAAA
TUG
RGH...
KCHING
BSHOOO

GAAH...
CRK
DAMN... JUST A GRAZE, AND THE FORCE WAS THAT STRONG...
HRG...
THUDD

VUMM
WHAT ?!!
BEHT BEHT

RA
AA
AA
WHUD
WHUD

AH!
SHIT! TWO AT ONCE ?!!
AAAAH!
WHUD

DOES DARKNESS HAVE NO EFFECT ON THE TITANS...?
OR IS IT THE SOUND...? OR SMELL?!

THE TITANS COME FROM THE SOUTH, LURED BY THE SMELL OF THEIR FOOD...
...AND GET STUCK AROUND SHIGANSHINA DISTRICT.

...!!
IT'S MY SMELL—THEIR FOOD.
RGH...

ZSH
YES, THEY'RE COMING THIS WAY...
CAN THEY SEE ME?!
SHMK
SHMK

WHUP
!!
THE FOOTSTEPS...
ARE APPROACHING?!

DO THREE, PAUSE, THEN THREE AGAIN TO GIVE THE PULL-UP SIGNAL.
FOUR OR MORE IN SUCCESSION MEANS AN EMERGENCY EXTRACTION.
KCHK
カチャ

OHH!
KCHAK
EVEN FROM THE TOP OF THE WALL, WE'LL BE ABLE TO SEE SPARKS ON THE GROUND AT NIGHT.
TWO SPARK SHOWERS WILL TELL US THAT YOU'VE LANDED SAFELY.
THESE SPARKS WILL SERVE AS A SIGNAL.
WHEN KUKLO GIVES THE SIGNAL, WE'LL SEND CARDINA DOWN.

WHEN YOU'RE ON THE GROUND, SEND A SIGNAL WITH THESE.
WE CAN'T USE SIGNAL FLARES, AS THIS IS A CLANDESTINE TEST.
IF THERE'S NO MOONLIGHT, WE CAN'T SEE BODY MOTIONS DOWN THERE.
WHAT ARE THEY ?
FLINT STONES.
USE THEM LIKE THIS.

DO I SEND A SIGNAL UP...?
A THREE-METER TITAN...200 METERS DIRECTLY SOUTH...
A FIVE-METER TITAN...300 METERS SOUTH-SOUTHWEST...

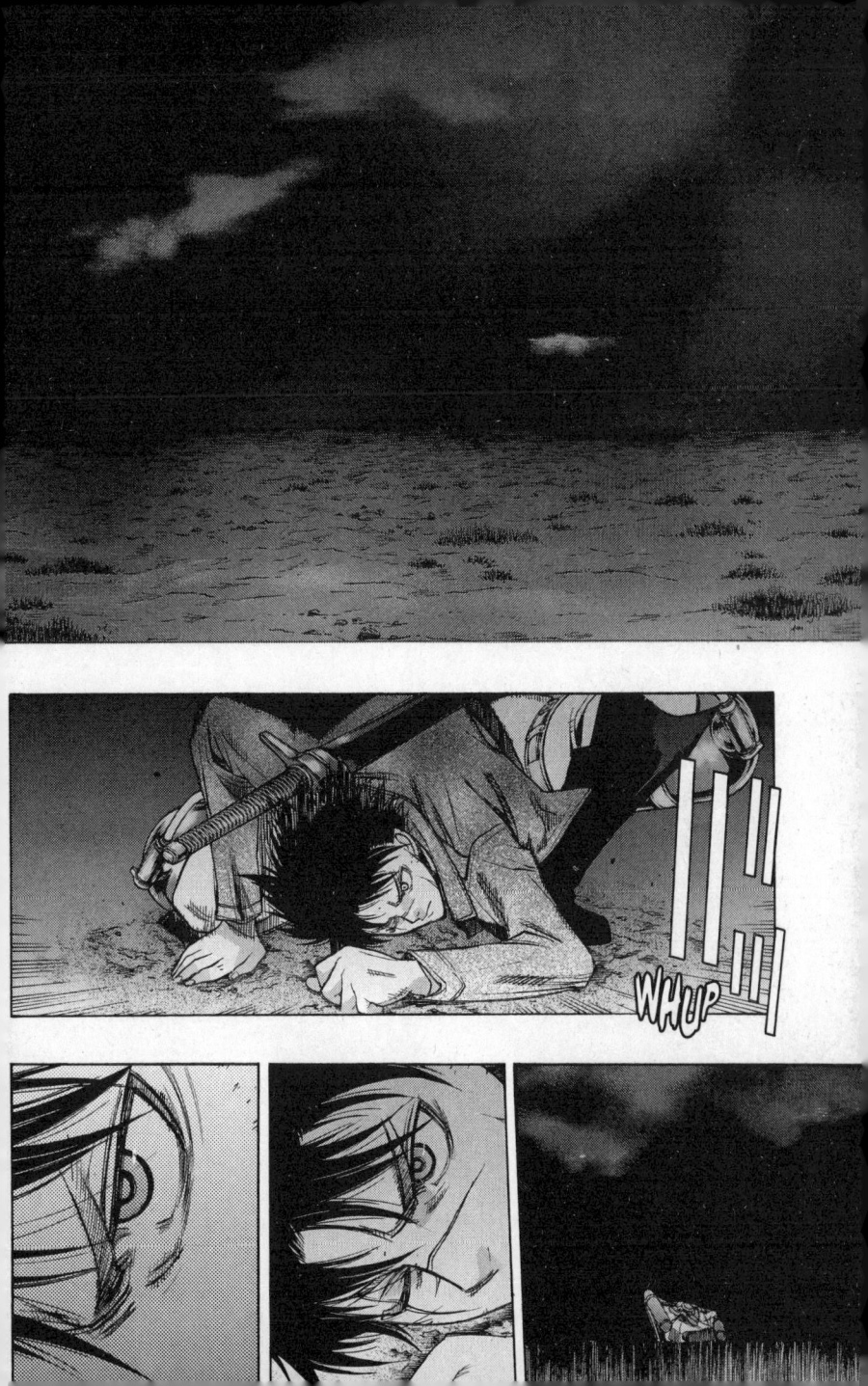
WHUP

Chapter 23: Rondo of Darkness

TUP
TUP
TUP

ATTACK ON TITAN

BEFORE THE FALL

Chapter 22: Abyss Below the Wall · End

SHAAA

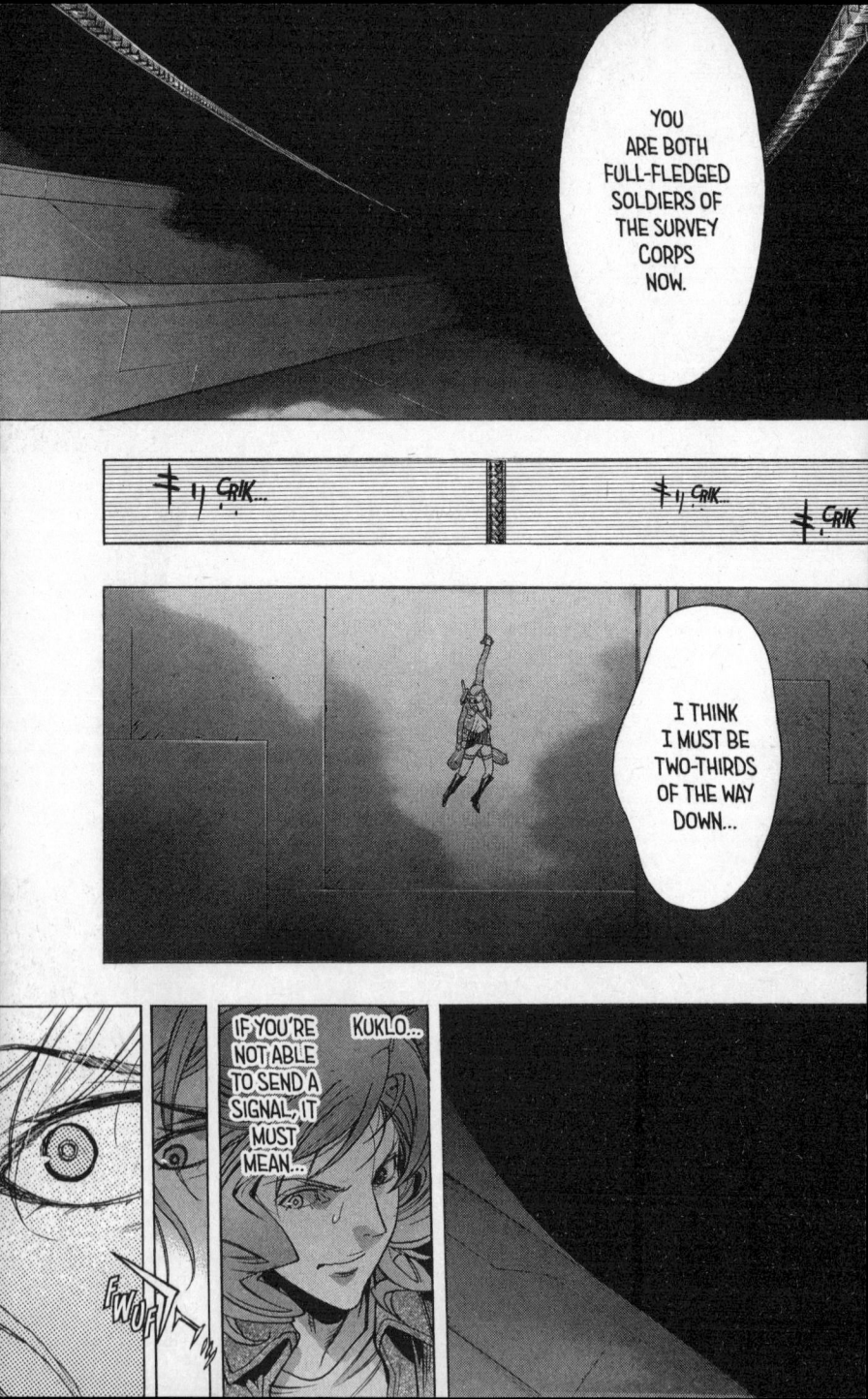
YOU ARE BOTH FULL-FLEDGED SOLDIERS OF THE SURVEY CORPS NOW.
CRIK...
CRIK...
CRIK
I THINK I MUST BE TWO-THIRDS OF THE WAY DOWN...
KUKLO...
IF YOU'RE NOT ABLE TO SEND A SIGNAL, IT MUST MEAN...
FWOF

THOSE BOYS ARE RISKING THEIR LIVES DOWN HERE...
...AND I CAN'T DO A THING FOR THEM...
YOU ARE THE "GUARDIAN DEITY OF WALL MARIA," AFTER ALL.
PRAY FOR THEIR SAFETY, THEN.
COME ON BACK...

...SO CAN YOU LOWER ME SLOWLY ?
OH!
BUT... I'M NOT AS NIMBLE WITH THIS AS KUKLO IS...
...ALL RIGHT.
DON'T WORRY, I'VE GOT YOU.
TE
TE
TRE
GRK...
GRK...

TE
TE
TE
TE
TE
E
TN
G!
SHR
EEE
E!
...NO SIGNAL..
HE SHOULD HAVE BEEN DOWN ON THE SURFACE BY NOW.
I... I'LL GO LOOK, TOO!

WHA...
I WILL GO, THEN.
TAP
TAP
...!
WHIRR
TONNNG

NOT FAR FROM DIRECTLY BELOW US... ONE...MAYBE TWO... NOT LARGE, I THINK.
THREE TO FIVE METERS, I'D GUESS.
GRIP
YOU CAN TELL ALL THAT JUST FROM THE SOUND ?!
IT'S TOO FAR FROM THE TOP OF THE WALL.
IT WILL BE CLEAR DOWN ON GROUND LEVEL.

I CAN TELL.
I CAN HEAR THEIR FOOTSTEPS.
!!

WHY?
I THINK YOU SHOULD CALL IT OFF TONIGHT.
YOU KNOW ...

YOU CAN'T SEE ANY DETAILS OF THE TERRAIN FIFTY METERS BELOW WITHOUT ANY MOONLIGHT.
THE WAY THE CLOUDS ARE HANGING LOW, WE MIGHT NOT GET A DECENT PATCH OF LIGHT AT ALL.

HMM...
I SUPPOSE WE HAVE NO CHOICE ...

OUR SQUAD'S NEXT NIGHT SHIFT IS IN SIX DAYS.
IF WE POST-PONE TONIGHT, WHEN WILL BE THE NEXT CHANCE ?

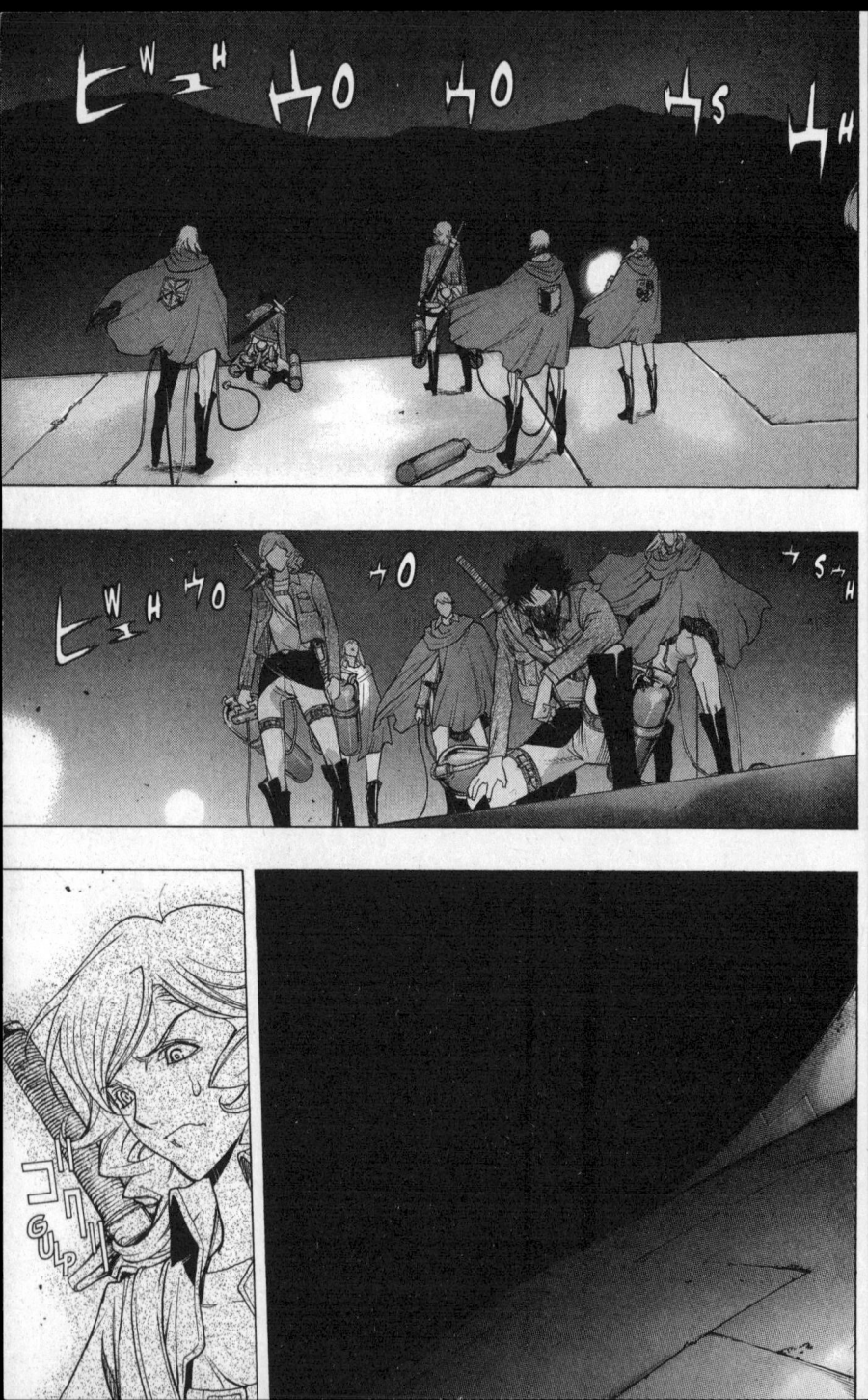
GULP

SH
KK
THAT'S WHAT WE'VE BEEN TRAINING TO ENSURE.
ALL THAT'S LEFT IS TO TEST IT IN THE FIELD!

IT'S GROWN IN SIZE QUITE A BIT FROM THE ORIGINAL...
IT'S NOT TOO HEAVY ?
WOOSH
XENOPHON SHAVED IT DOWN AS MUCH AS HE COULD AFFORD, BUT IT'S STILL TWICE THE WEIGHT OF THE OLD DEVICE.
WILL YOU HAVE ENOUGH MOBILITY ?

LOOK AT THAT!
IS IT... A NEW MODEL?

CLANK
PSHT
PSHT
KTHUNK

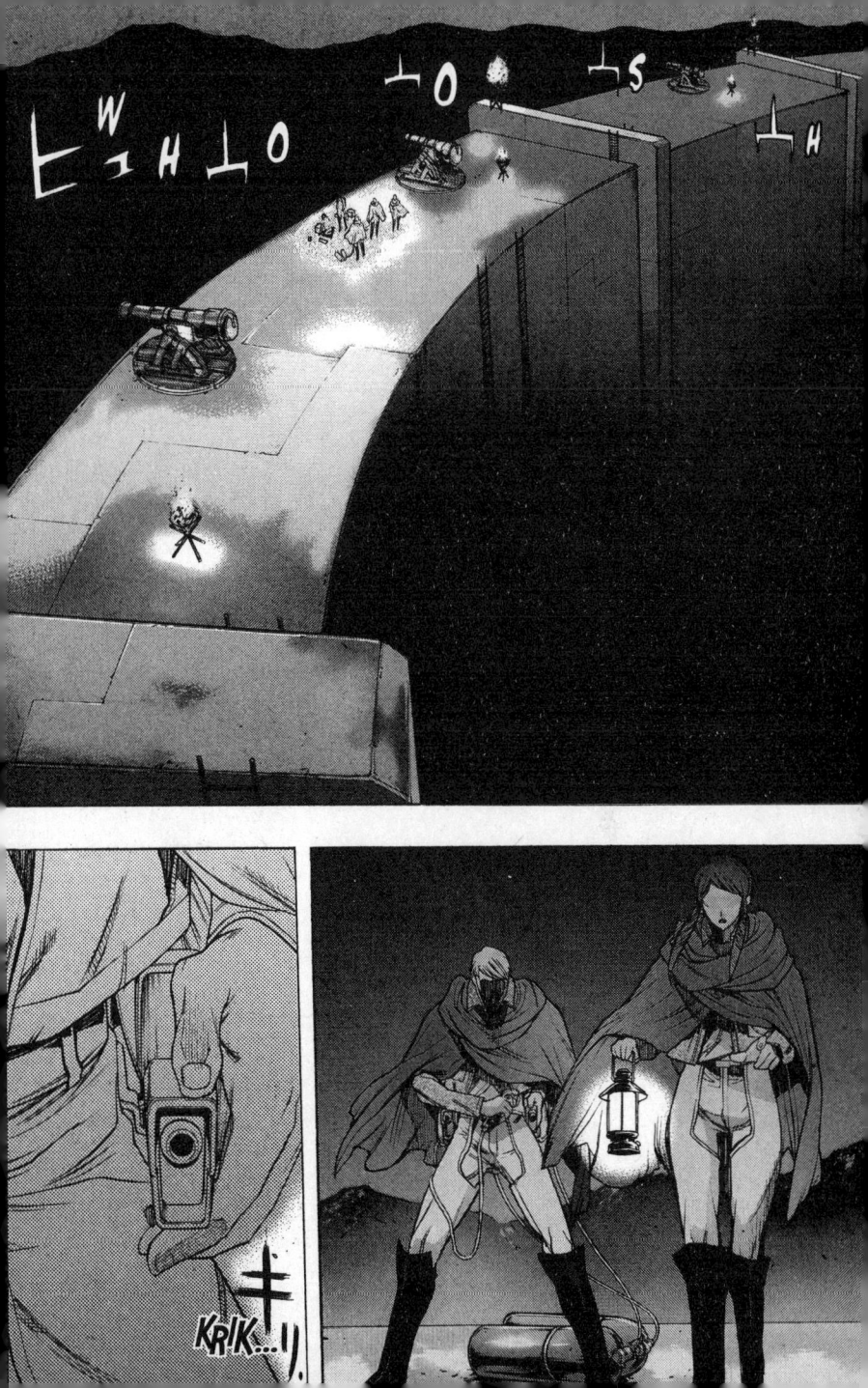
KRIK...

IF ONLY MY DAUGHTER WERE AS SWEET AS YOU!
HUH?
YOU HAVE A DAUGHTER ?
YES, SORUM'S CHILD.
SHE'S ABOUT YOUR AGE.
THEY SAY A CHILD NEVER UNDERSTANDS A PARENT'S PAINS. SHE APPLIED TO THE SURVEY CORPS, AGAINST MY WISHES.
ANYWAY...
TRY NOT TO MAKE TOO MUCH NOISE. OUR SQUAD IS THE ONLY ONE OF THE GARRISON CORPS IN ON THIS LITTLE STUNT.

WHUP
TH...
THANK YOU SO MUCH !!
OH, IT'S FINE, IT'S FINE.
DON'T MAKE A BIG DEAL OUT OF IT.

HELPING PEOPLE IS A BIT OF AN INGRAINED HABIT.
IN FACT, WHEN I WAS YOUNGER, I WAS KNOWN AS "THE GUARDIAN DEITY OF WALL MARIA."

?
BUT... YOU ARE YOUNG.
OOH!
YOU DO KNOW HOW TO TALK TO A LADY, KUKLO!

WHO IS
!
SHE WAS ONCE SORUM HUMÉ'S FIANCÉE.
I WAS ALSO LONGTIME FRIENDS WITH ANGEL.
THE ONE WHO BLEW HIMSELF UP TO TAKE DOWN MAMMON...
OF COURSE I'M GOING TO HELP YOU WITH IT.
THAT DEVICE IS LIKE THE DREAM OF THOSE FOOLISH BOYS, PUT INTO PHYSICAL FORM.
!
WHEN WE RESCUED YOU FROM YOUR EXILE, SHE WAS THE ONE WHO HELPED PULL THE STRINGS.

AND I'M GUESSING YOU'RE CARDINA.
...?
?
BUT WHO ARE YOU ...?
Y...YES, THAT'S ME...
!
CARLO TOLD ME ABOUT YOU TWO.
I'M MARIA CARLSTEAD OF THE GARRISON CORPS.
YOU'RE GOING TO USE ANGEL'S DEVICE, RIGHT?

YOU MUST BE KUKLO.
NICE TO MEET YOU.

WHAM
AHH!
HUFF!
HUFF!
CARLO!
YOU'RE PRETTY OUT-OF-BREATH YOURSELF, DAD.
CUT THE ELDERLY SOME SLACK, WOULD YOU?!
HUFF!
SEEMS LIKE YOU TWO COULD USE A LITTLE MORE MUSCLE TRAINING.
HUFF!
I'VE BEEN WAITING FOR YOU BOYS.

CREAK
CREAK
WHOOSH
AH...
H-HYA...
CREAK
CREAK

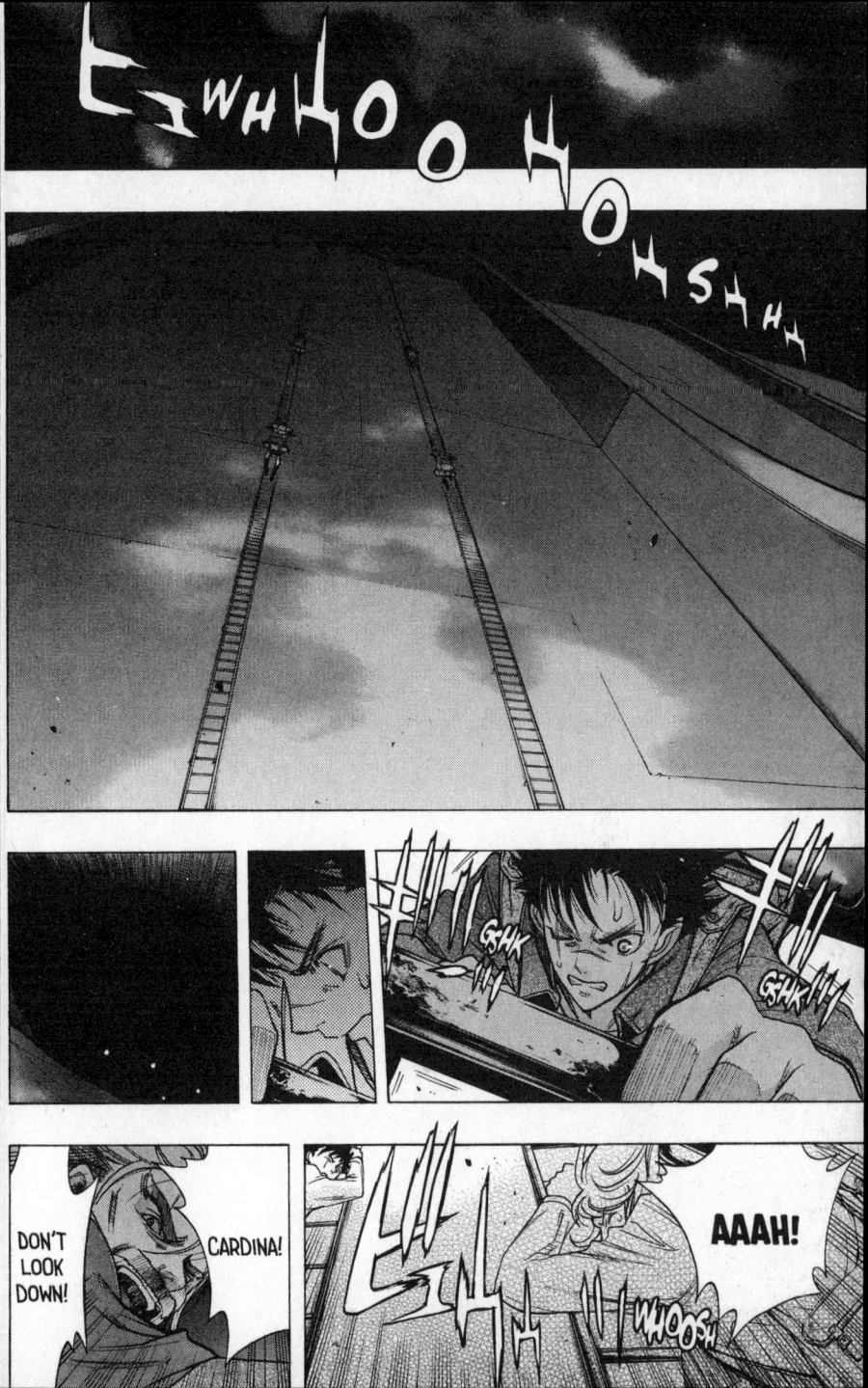
WHOOOOOSHH
GSHK
GSHK
DON'T LOOK DOWN!
CARDINA!
AAAH!
WHOOSH

WILL YOU BE ALL RIGHT ?
I WAS JUST STARTING TO NOD OFF WHEN IT CAME TIME TO GO.
NO, I CAUGHT A FEW WINKS EARLIER IN THE DAY, WHILE WE WERE IN THE CART.
!
...GOOD TO KNOW.
OH, I'M JUST FINE!!
WHEN CARDINA BAUMEISTER SETS HIS MIND TO IT, HE CAN DO ANYTHING!
LET'S GO!
CLANK
LOOKS LIKE THE DEAL IS DONE.
CLANK

WHAT, YOU DIDN'T GET MUCH SLEEP?
FWAAAH!

FSP
FSCH

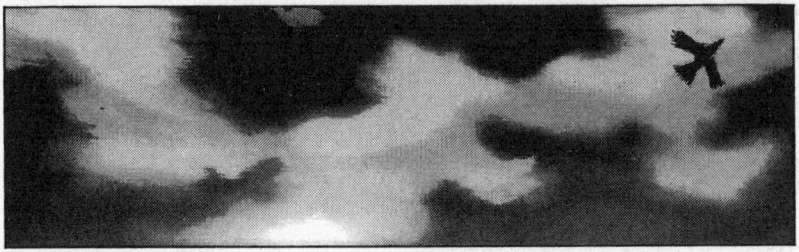

SO THAT... THERE CAN BE ANOTHER EXPEDI-TION?
NATURALLY.
HUMANITY HAS NO HOPE WITHIN THESE WALLS. PLUS...
IF WE STOP NOW, THOSE WHO HAVE ALREADY GIVEN THEIR LIVES WILL NEVER SEE THEIR SACRIFICE PAY OFF.
...

NORMALLY, THE CORPS WOULD NOT RUBBER-STAMP EVERY TRANSFER REQUEST LIKE THIS...
BUT ONCE THEY HAVE LOST THEIR WILL TO PARTICIPATE, THEY ARE NO USE TO US HERE.
OH... I SEE.
THAT'S WHY YOU WERE THERE...
SO DAD'S BEEN OUT DRUMMING UP SUPPORT AND RECRUITING NEW MEMBERS.
THE SITUATION IS SO DIRE...
...THAT EVEN JORGE THE HERO IS FORCED TO RUN COMMON ERRANDS TO MAKE ENDS MEET!!

THERE ARE SO FEW PEOPLE HERE...
KUKLO!

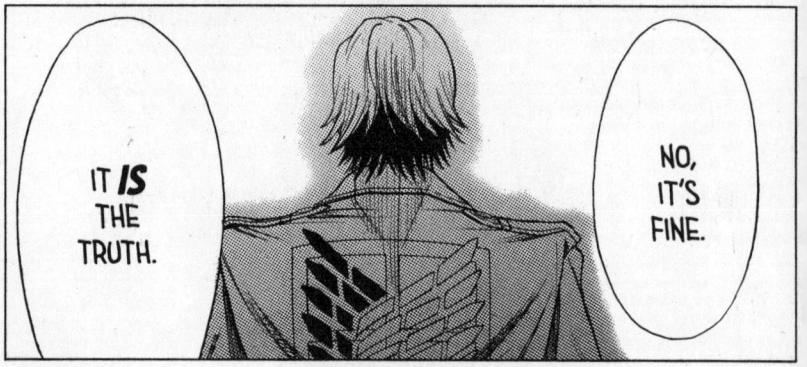
NO, IT'S FINE.
IT IS THE TRUTH.

EVER SINCE THE LAST EXPEDITION, MORE AND MORE OF OUR NUMBER HAVE SUBMITTED TRANSFER REQUESTS.
MOST OF THEM HAD THEIR WILLS BROKEN BY THAT FIRSTHAND ENCOUNTER WITH THE TITAN MENACE...
AND THOSE WHO DIDN'T TAKE PART IN THE TRIP HAVE LITTLE FAITH IN THE FUTURE OF THE SURVEY CORPS.

I DO HAVE A MEANS ARRANGED TO REACH THE TOP OF WALL MARIA...
...BUT WITHOUT OFFICIAL PERMISSION, WE'LL HAVE TO DO IT IN THE DEAD OF NIGHT.
JUST REST AND RELAX UNTIL THEN.
FORTUNATELY, WE HAVE PLENTY OF EMPTY ROOMS.

Y-YES, SIR!
HA HA HA! I'LL GET A CHANCE TO SEE YOUR ACTUAL SKILL IN THE FLESH, THEN.
COME IN, AND I'LL HAVE YOU FED IN NO TIME!
WELL, I EXPECT YOU HAVEN'T EATEN YET, CORRECT?!

I AM CARDINA BAUMEISTER!
I, TOO, WISH TO JOIN THE SURVEY CORPS!

CARLO PIKALE.
AS CAPTAIN OF THE SURVEY CORPS, I WELCOME YOU!

N-NO, SIR... I DIDN'T EVEN GRADUATE, I'M AFRAID...

HUH?
MY FATHER TOLD ME ABOUT YOU.
APPARENTLY YOU HAD QUITE EXCELLENT MARKS IN TRAINING.

HE SAID THEY "STOOD ON THE BRINK OF DEATH TOGETHER"...
PERHAPS THAT'S WHAT IT MEANS.

I'M JEALOUS OF KUKLO...
...THAT HE HAS SUCH A COMPANION.

...!
OH, PARDON ME.

UM...

THE VETERAN SOLDIER, CAPTAIN CARLO PIKALE...
...IS THE ONE BEARING THE BLOOD OF THE GREAT HERO JORGE...
...HE'S NOT WHAT I EXPECTED...
BUT FOR BEING A VETERAN OF BATTLE...
NO...

HMM?
FOR SAVING ME FROM MY PUNISHMENT OF EXILE...
I ALWAYS WANTED TO THANK YOU.
SO THIS MAN...
HA HA HA
WHAT A THING TO SAY ABOUT THE SENIOR CITIZEN YOU ABUSE LEFT AND RIGHT!
KNOCK IT OFF.
THEN AGAIN, DON'T THANK DAD—HE WANTED TO RECRUIT YOU FOR THE SURVEY CORPS ALL ALONG.
I DID NOTHING. IF YOU WANT TO THANK ANYONE, THANK MISS SHARLE AND MY DAD.

HA...
HA HA HA HA HA HA!
HA HA!
AHA HA HA HA!
HA HA HA HA HA!
AHA HA HA HA HA!
HA HA!
...HA...
YEAH ...
HA HA...
HA HA HA... AHHH... WE STOOD ON THE BRINK OF DEATH TOGETHER, AND SOMEHOW NEVER INTRODUCED OURSELVES.
THANK YOU...

KUKLO...
HOPEFUL RECRUIT OF THE SURVEY CORPS.
...SIR.
PFF!

CARLO PIKALE.
AS YOU MAY KNOW, I AM CAPTAIN OF THE SURVEY CORPS.

I FINALLY SEE YOU'RE SAFE AND SOUND.
HELLO THERE, YOUNGSTER.
ZSHH
I NEVER GOT THE CHANCE TO PROPERLY INTRODUCE MYSELF.
AH...

THUNK
THUNK
IT WAS ONLY A FEW MONTHS AGO...BUT IT FEELS LIKE THE DISTANT PAST.
WHAT DOES?
I LIVED HERE...WITH SHARLE...
KUKLO, CARDINA! ALL CLEAR!!

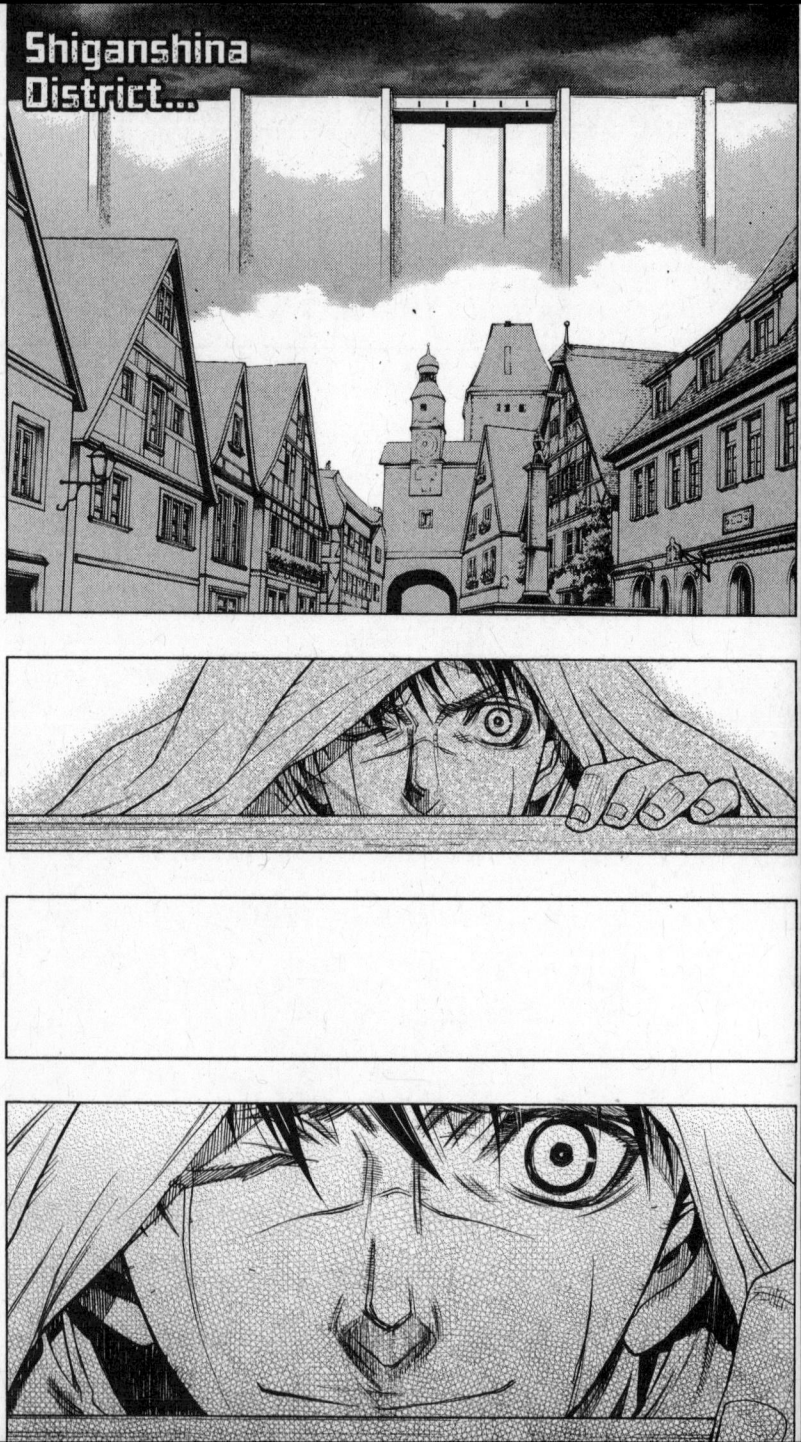
Shiganshina
District...

AHHH! WE'VE FINALLY MADE IT TO SHIGANSHINA DISTRICT!
PWAH!!
YOU WILL STILL ATTRACT ATTENTION HERE IN TOWN.
SWISH
STAY PUT UNTIL WE REACH THE SURVEY CORPS BARRACKS.

...JORGE THE HERO...
I UNDER-STAND HOW YOU FEEL, BUT YOU'RE ON DUTY!
Y-YES, SIR!!
HEY! GET BACK TO WORK, DAMMIT!
I WAS IN A DIFFERENT TRAINING BARRACK... THAT'S THE FIRST TIME I'VE EVER SEEN HIM! THE MAN WHO DEFEATED A TITAN...
ON TO THE NEXT!!
NEXT!

PLEASE COME THROUGH !!
WHAP
WELCOME BACK, INSTRUCTOR PIKALE!!
RATTLE
RATTLE
RATTLE
SO THAT'S...
RATTLE
RATTLE
RATTLE
...

Chapter 22: Abyss Below the Wall

ATTACK ON TITAN

BEFORE THE FALL

Chapter 21: Den of Treachery · End

ゴト
KHUNK
KHUNK
ゴト
KHUNK
ゴト

THE MAN I SENT INTO THE CITY SHOULD BE ABLE TO FIND SHARLE WITHOUT MUCH TROUBLE.
A YOUNG WOMAN LIKE HER IS BOUND TO STICK OUT IN THAT PLACE.
THAT BERNHART VIXEN THINKS SHE CAN USE ME TO HER ENDS, BUT THIS ULTIMATELY BENEFITS ME MORE THAN HER.
NOW I WILL HAVE BOTH SHARLE BACK AND BERNHART'S WEAKNESS TO MY ADVANTAGE.
YES, I'LL DO IT...
FOR I AM THE MAN WHO CONQUERED A TITAN!

PERHAPS IT'S TRUE, AND KUKLO REALLY HAD NO CONNECTION TO THE WORSHIPPERS AFTER ALL...

IN THAT CASE, I HAVE A SUGGES-TION.

THE OLD MASTER HAD A CONNECTION AMONG THE WORKERS WHO TRANSPORT CORPS EQUIPMENT TO THE INDUSTRIAL CITY.
I SUGGEST THAT WE CALL UPON A FAVOR AND HAVE A CARRIAGE SPECIALLY OUTFITTED TO SNEAK SOMEONE INTO THE CITY.

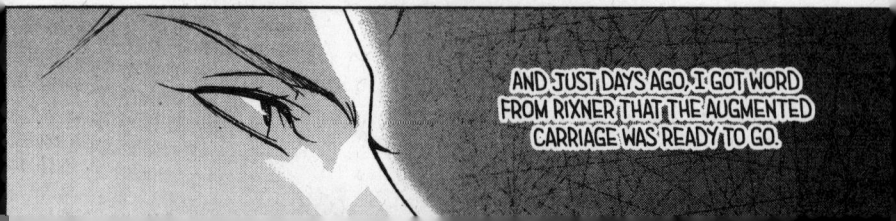
AND JUST DAYS AGO, I GOT WORD FROM RIXNER THAT THE AUGMENTED CARRIAGE WAS READY TO GO.

IF SHE WAS GOING TO SEND HIM AT ALL, HE'D BE THE PROXY AND I WOULD BE THE AIDE.
BASED ON THE "SECRET MISSION" CAPTAIN BERNHART ASSIGNED TO ME...
MATTEUS IS AN OBSERVER TO ENSURE THE MISSION SUCCEEDS...
...AND POSSIBLY THERE TO FINISH ME OFF, IF NECESSARY.
...SHE MIGHT WANT TO MAKE ME THE FALL GUY—THE LIZARD'S TAIL SHE CAN CUT LOOSE IF ANYTHING GOES WRONG.
BUT...
I DIDN'T GET ANYTHING FROM THE TITAN-WOR-SHIPPERS, AND I'M OUT OF CLUES TO FOLLOW SHARLE, TOO.
IT ALSO SUITS MY ENDS TO BE ABLE TO GET INTO THE INDUSTRIAL CITY AT THIS POINT IN TIME.

ゴト
KTHUNK
ゴト
KTHUNK
ゴト
KTHUNK
ゴト
KTHUNK

ガラ RATTLE
RATTLE ガラ
ガラ RATTLE
ガラ RATTLE
RATTLE ガラ

CRIKK
コキ!

THAT'S ALL FOR THE HARKIMO WORKSHOP. JUST SIGN THIS FORM.
DONE AND DONE.

CREAK...

I HAVE A FEELING THAT MISS SHARLE WILL BE PULLING OUT ALL THE STOPS FOR THIS ONE. I CAN'T WAIT.
!
I HEAR YOU LOUD AND CLEAR!
IT'S BEEN TOO LONG SINCE I HAD A CHANCE TO REALLY TEST MY COOKING SKILL!!
THAT'S THE LAST ONE!
DON'T GET SLOPPY !
AND... THERE WE GO!

WITH THAT SAID, WE'RE LEAVING FOR SHIGANSHINA DISTRICT AT THE BREAK OF DAWN TOMORROW!
KUKLO AND CARDINA, MAKE ALL OF YOUR PREPARATIONS FOR THE TRIP TONIGHT!
SHARLE.
IS THIS ACCEPTABLE, FOREMAN?
OF COURSE.
I'LL PERFORM A FINAL TUNE-UP ON THE NEW DEVICE.
NO NEED TO WORK TODAY. WHIP UP A GOOD FEAST FOR DINNER INSTEAD.
A BIG PARTY TO WELCOME INSTRUCTOR PIKALE AND SEND OFF KUKLO AND CARDINA.

AS IF THAT STOPPED ME BEFORE !!
...THAT'S THE SPIRIT!

BUT THE TEST WILL BE AGAINST A TITAN.
AND DEPENDING ON THE CIRCUMSTANCES, POSSIBLY MORE THAN ONE.
THIS TEST WILL PUT YOUR LIVES AT RISK.

THE DEVICE DOESN'T HAVE TO BE PERFECT FROM THE VERY START!
ISN'T IT OUR JOB TO TEST IT IN THE FIELD TO FIND OUT HOW WE CAN IMPROVE IT?!
THAT TAKES A BIG LOAD OFF OF MY SHOULDERS, SON. THANK YOU.
I'LL NEED YOU TO BRING ME GOOD TEST DATA, KUKLO AND CARDINA.
CREAK

IN ESSENCE, EVERYTHING I'VE DONE IS JUST A RE-PACKAGING...
...OF THE TECHNOLOGY THAT ANGEL BROUGHT FORTH YEARS AGO.
AND THE RESULT IS THIS RATHER UNGAINLY THING...
...
A TRULY EXCELLENT MACHINE HAS THE ELEGANT, BEAUTIFUL FORM TO MATCH.
IN THAT SENSE, THIS "NEW DEVICE" IS STILL INCOMPLETE...
BUT THE PRACTICAL TEST IS MEANT TO IDENTIFY THOSE FLAWS, RIGHT?

FOR NOW...
...I THINK THAT THIS IS THE FINEST MODEL I CAN MAKE AT PRESENT.
TO BE HONEST... I'VE COME TO REALIZE THE LIMITS OF MY IMAGINATION.
THAT'S NOT THE PROUD ENDORSEMENT I'VE COME TO EXPECT FROM YOU, HARKIMO.

IT SHOULD BE POSSIBLE TO DO A PRACTICAL TEST OF THE DEVICE NOW.
...!
CLENCH
AND HOW GOES THE REFINING OF THE DEVICE?

INDEED.
HAVE YOU DETERMINED THAT THE CHASE HAS COOLED OFF?
IF YOU'RE HERE, THAT MEANS YOU'VE COME TO TAKE US WITH YOU, RIGHT?
THE LAST OF THE TITAN-WORSHIPPERS WERE FINALLY WIPED OUT IN SHIGANSHINA DISTRICT JUST RECENTLY.
I DOUBT ANYONE IS GOING TO DIG UP AND REEXAMINE THE DEATH OF THE TITAN'S SON.
THAT MEANS THE MP BRIGADE'S SEARCH FOR THE WORSHIPPERS WILL CALM DOWN NOW.
THEN...

IT'S BEEN A WHILE.
THREE AND A HALF MONTHS SINCE WE LAST MET, I BELIEVE.
YEAH!!
I'VE BEEN WAITING!
NEARLY DIED WAITING, IN FACT!

!
INSTRUCTOR JORGE!!

HARKIMO WORKSHOP HANDLES JUST TWENTY BOXES OF GEAR FROM WALL SHEENA.
EVEN THAT'S QUITE A LOT TO DEAL WITH, THOUGH...
AHA! IN FACT, THIS MIGHT BE GOOD PRACTICE FOR YOU, SHARLE.
ME ??!
ARE YOU SURE?
I'LL PICK OUT THE EASY ONES SO YOU DON'T GET OVER-WHELMED.
KLOW AND CARL, YOU HELP UNLOAD THE BOXES.
I'M NOT REALLY CUT OUT FOR HEAVY LIFTING...
SWOOSH...
YOU LOOK BUSY.

WHAT IS IT?
I ALWAYS HATE TO HAVE TO PAUSE DEVELOPMENT FOR THIS.
GREAT, IT'S THIS PERIOD AGAIN.
IT DOESN'T TAKE LONG, WHAT WITH THE TALENTED FOLKS I KEEP...
EQUIPMENT MAINTENANCE FOR THE CORPS. THEY SEND IT ALL ONCE A QUARTER.
...THERE'S JUST TOO MUCH OF IT!
SCRATCH
SCRATCH
IF WE TOOK ALL OF IT, WE'D HAVE NO TIME FOR DEVELOPMENT TO BEGIN WITH!
OH, NO!
ALL OF THE CORPS' EQUIPMENT IS HANDLED AT THIS WORKSHOP ?

SORRY, SIR! WE'RE GETTING BACK TO WORK!!
R-RIGHT, SIR!

CLUNKA
BUT THE REGULATIONS STATE -!
YOU KNOW THAT THE INDUSTRIAL CITY PROVIDES THE EQUIPMENT AND MAINTENANCE FOR ALL THE DIFFERENT DISTRICT FORCES, RIGHT?
THESE ONES ARE FINE.
CLUNKA
CLUNKA
CLUNKA
CLUNKA
CLUNKA
THESE CARRIAGES REGULARLY BRING WEAPONS AND ARMOR THAT NEED REPAIRS TO THE WORKSHOPS HERE IN THE INDUSTRIAL CITY.
YOU TWO! ENJOYING YOUR CHAT?!
BECAUSE YOU NEED TO GET BACK TO YOUR STATIONS AND MAN THE GATE!!
CLUNKA
CLUNKA
CLUNKA
AND WE KNOW ALL THE DRIVERS, SO THERE ARE NO ISSUES WITH IDENTITY.
WE USED TO TRANSFER EVERYTHING TO THE WORKSHOP CARRIAGES AT THE GATE, BUT IT TOOK SO MUCH TIME AND LABOR THAT THE CAPTAIN AUTHORIZED US TO JUST LET THEM THROUGH.

ALL RIGHT! YOU'RE FREE TO GO!
CLUNKA
CLUNKA
CLUNKA
CLUNKA
CLUNKA
CLUNKA
HUH?
WAIT, YOU'RE JUST GOING TO LET THOSE CARRIAGES FROM OUTSIDE PASS THROUGH?
OH, RIGHT! YOU'RE NEW HERE.

ザワ MURMUR
MURMUR ザワ

KNOWING YOUR TALENTS, XAVI, I HAVE A REQUEST OF YOU.

YOU'RE JOKING, MA'AM!
HE MIGHT EVEN TAKE A LIKING TO YOU. TRY NOT TO BE WON OVER TO HIS SIDE.
HE WILL NOT MIND THAT I'VE SENT A PROXY.
PLUS, HE FANCIES HIMSELF A MAN OF THE PEOPLE.
BUT IN THAT CASE, I WILL GLADLY TAKE ON THIS DUTY FOR YOU!
!
YOUR REAL MISSION IS AS FOLLOWS.
BUT THAT IS JUST FOR OUTWARD APPEARANCES.

DO YOU KNOW THAT MY UNCLE IS BAUDUIN BERNHART, VICE COMMANDER OF THE MILITARY POLICE?
WHEN MY PLACEMENT IN SHIGANSHINA WAS DECIDED, I HAD RIXNER COMPILE THE PERSONAL HISTORIES AND BACKGROUNDS OF ALL THE MEMBERS HERE.
YES, MA'AM!
!
AND YOU KNOW THAT MY UNCLE AND CAPTAIN DAFNER ARE RIVALS TO THE POSITION OF THE FUTURE MP COMMANDER?
NATURALLY, I AM SEEN AS A MEMBER OF THE BERNHART FACTION.
YES.
IT'S STILL UNDER WRAPS, SEE. THE INDUSTRIAL CITY MPS HAVE ALWAYS HAD AN INDEPENDENT STREAK THAT PUTS THEM AT ODDS WITH CENTRAL.
I... HAD NOT HEARD THIS.

NEXT WEEK, YOU WILL VISIT THE INDUSTRIAL CITY AS MY PROXY.
YES.
THUMP
NEXT... MISSION ?
THE INDUSTRIAL CITY!!
!
DON'T WORRY, YOU'RE ONLY REQUESTING FRESH EQUIPMENT. IT'S JUST PAYING RESPECTS.
OH. THAT?
BUT...HOW CAN A NEW RECRUIT LIKE ME SERVE AS A CAPTAIN'S PROXY?
I... SEE...
...?
I DON'T THINK HE'LL BE EAGER TO SEE ME IN PERSON.
THE TASK IS A SIMPLE FORMALITY...BUT CAPTAIN DAFNER OF THE INDUSTRIAL CITY AND I DON'T GET ALONG.

SO THAT MARKS THE END OF THE LUNATICS WHO HELPED THE TITAN INVADE FIFTEEN YEARS AGO...
YOU MUST BE SATISFIED TO HAVE AVENGED YOUR FATHER'S DEATH.
NO! I AM PERSONALLY DEALING WITH THE MAN WHO SLAUGHTERED MY FATHER. IT WAS COMPLETELY OBJECTIVE THIS TIME.
I WAS MERELY DOING MY DUTY AS AN MP.
I SEE. PUT TOGETHER YOUR REPORT AND SUBMIT IT TO ME, THEN.
Y-
YES, MA'AM !!
KTHUNK
WAIT. I NEED TO TELL YOU ABOUT YOUR NEXT MISSION FIRST.

...YES.
THANK YOU, MA'AM.
IF THEY EVER GIVE YOU ANY TROUBLE AGAIN, PLEASE TELL ME OR MY AIDE, LENZ.
...!
YES, MA'AM !!
BUT ENOUGH ABOUT THAT. PLEASE GIVE ME YOUR REPORT.
ACCORDING TO THEIR PRIEST, THEY WERE THE LAST OF THE TITAN-WORSHIPPERS IN SHIGANSHINA.
NATURALLY, WE WILL NEED TO THOROUGHLY INVESTIGATE THOSE HE IS CONNECTED TO...
...BUT I SUSPECT THAT THIS OPERATION HAS SUCCEEDED IN WIPING OUT THE TITAN-WORSHIPPERS.

!
FORTY-FIVE YEARS, MANKIND HAS BEEN TRAPPED BEHIND THESE WALLS.

IT HAS BECOME A NEST OF SLOTH AND SELF-INTEREST, FILLED ONLY WITH THOSE WHO SCORED HIGHLY IN THE TRAINING CORPS IN ORDER TO GAIN A LIFETIME OF JOB SECURITY.
AT FIRST, THE MILITARY POLICE WERE CHOSEN FROM THE BEST TO PROVIDE ORDER AND SAFETY TO A POPULACE FALLEN INTO CHAOS AND TERROR. NOW, THEY ARE ELITE IN NAME ONLY.

SOME OF THE OFFICERS RECOGNIZE YOUR TALENT AND LOFTY AMBITION.
...IT IS NOT ***ONLY*** THOSE WHO SEEK TO PUNISH YOU FOR NOT SHARING IN THEIR VICE.
HOW-EVER...

I AM ONE OF THEM.

NO, MA'AM, I DIDN'T MEAN TO IMPLY...
OR DO YOU THINK I'M THE KIND OF SHAMELESS WOMAN WHO WOULD PEEP INTO THE MEN'S WASHING STATION?

SMIRK
ニヤ
SMIRK
ニヤ
HMM?
Y-YOU AREN'T...GOING TO PUNISH ME FOR WHAT JUST HAPPENED?
...NO...
DID YOU DO SOMETHING THAT REQUIRES PUNISHMENT?
FOR WHAT?

YOU MUST BE TIRED. SIT DOWN.
YES, MA'AM!
THANK YOU VERY MUCH!
SWISH
I WILL SIT NOW! PARDON ME!

ACK
ギク!!
WHAKK
GOOD MORNING, XAVI.
YOU DID GOOD WORK OUT THERE, EXPOSING THE TITAN-WORSHIPPERS' HIDEOUT AND QUESTIONING THE LEADER ALL NIGHT.
TH-THANK YOU, MA'AM, BUT IT WAS NOTHING!
I HATE TO BOTHER YOU WHEN YOU COULD USE SOME REST, BUT COULD YOU COME TO MY OFFICE?
BEFORE YOU SUBMIT YOUR REPORT, I WANT TO HEAR WHAT THE RING-LEADER SAID, RIGHT FROM YOUR OWN MOUTH.

CREAK
キィ
SHARP
THANK YOU FOR YOUR INSTRUCTION.
UGH

WE'RE SICK AND TIRED OF YOU SHOWING OFF LIKE THIS!!
I'M TALKIN' TO YOU, INOCENCIO !!
WHAT MAKES YOU TAKE THAT ATTITUDE WHEN A SENIOR IS TAKIN' TIME OUT OF HIS DAY TO SPEAK TO YOU?!
SIGH
I BET YOU PAID OFF THE OFFICERS TO FINISH YOUR TRAINING CORPS REGIMEN EARLY!!
WELL, WE'RE GONNA FINISH YOUR EDUCATION!!

YOU SUGGESTED YOURSELF FOR THE JOB, THEN TORTURED HIM? I LIKE YOUR STYLE, NEW GUY.
PTU
YOU HAVE FUN TORTURING A MAN, YOUNG MASTER?
HYA HA HA!
SPLASH
...!

SPLISH
SPLISH
I HEAR YOU PUT ON QUITE A SHOW OUT THERE.

VERY WELL. HE'S ALL YOURS.
THANK YOU, MA'AM!!

GOOD! OPERATION COMPLETE !!
ALL UNITS WITHDRAW!
SEND THE RINGLEADER TO THE INTERROGATION ROOM!
I HAVE A REQUEST, CAPTAIN BERNHART!
DO YOU THINK I COULD QUESTION THIS MAN?!
YOU'RE JUST THE NEW GUY! WHAT DO YOU THINK GIVES YOU THE RIGHT TO—

WELL DONE, INOCENCIO!
SO WE'VE GOT THE RINGLEADER. WHAT ABOUT HIS DISCIPLES?
THAT MATCHES THE NUMBER THAT FLED FROM THEIR HIDEOUT.
THREE DEAD IN ALL...

HUH?!
I'VE CAPTURED THE HEAD OF THE TITAN-WORSHIPPERS !!
I AM XAVI INOCENCIO, SQUAD THREE!
THE MOMENT THEY HEAR A GUNSHOT, THEY COME CARELESSLY RUNNING! SO THIS IS THE BEST THE MPs CAN DO NOWADAYS...
...!!

GUH...
AH...
AH... GAH!
GRRK
DMM
THE SHOT CAME FROM OVER HERE!
STOMP STOMP

GWANG!

DA DUM
BSH

YOU CANNOT COVER UP THE STENCH OF ROTTING FILTH.
I WILL ALWAYS BE ABLE TO SNIFF YOU OUT.
DASH!!!

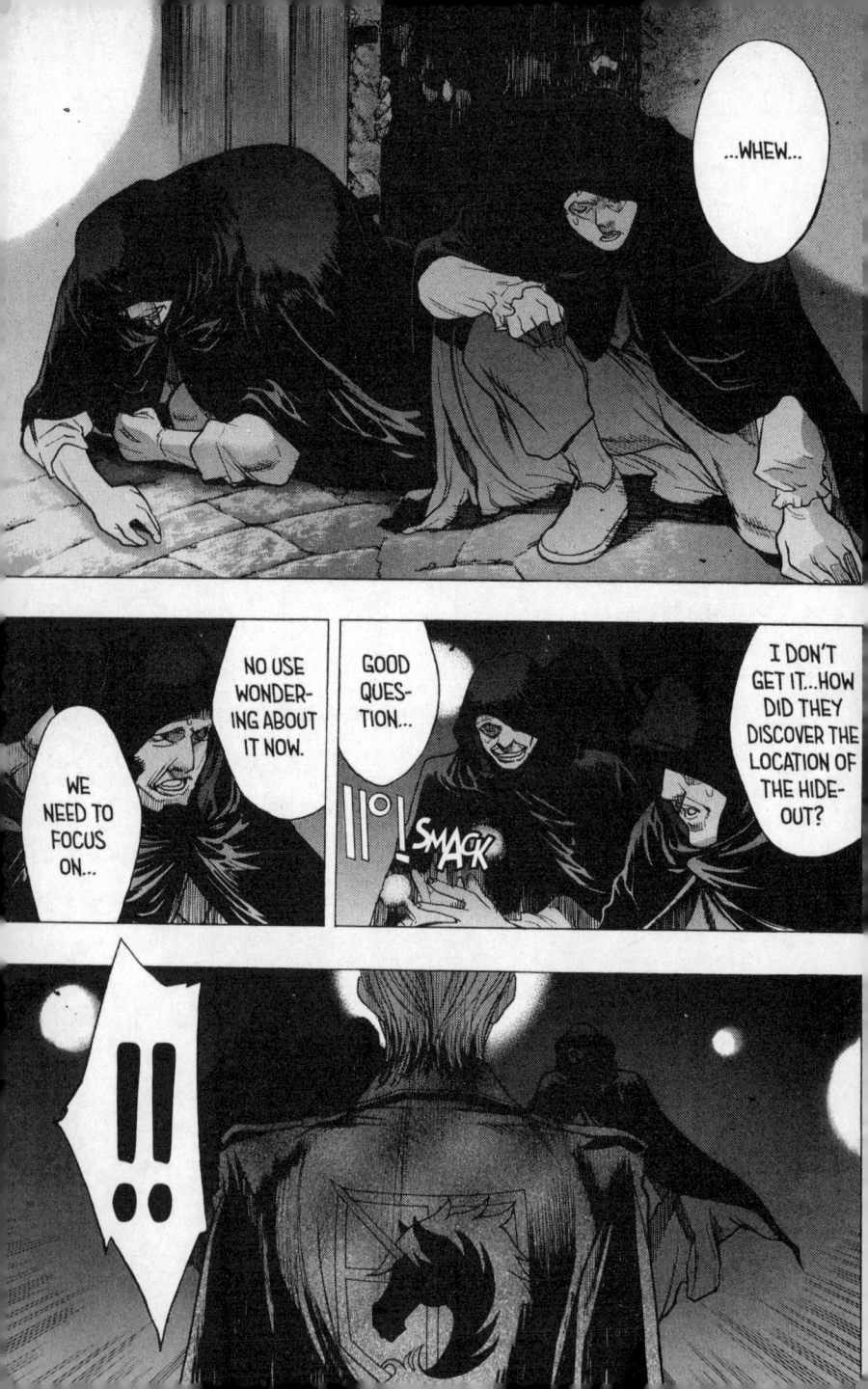
...WHEW...
I DON'T GET IT...HOW DID THEY DISCOVER THE LOCATION OF THE HIDE-OUT?
GOOD QUES-TION...
!!°!
SMACK
NO USE WONDER-ING ABOUT IT NOW.
WE NEED TO FOCUS ON...
!!

The Story So Far

When a Titan terrorized Shiganshina District and left behind a pile of vomit, a baby boy was miraculously born of a pregnant corpse. This boy was named Kuklo, the "Titan's Son," and treated as a sideshow freak. Eventually the wealthy merchant Dario Inocencio bought Kuklo to serve as a punching bag for his son, Xavi. Meanwhile, Xavi's sister Sharle decided to teach him the language and knowledge of humanity instead. Kuklo put together an escape plan over two long years, but on the day of the escape, a group of Titan-worshippers invaded the mansion to take back the "Titan's Son," and murdered Dario in the process. Kuklo narrowly managed to save Sharle, but Xavi accused him of being in league with the attackers. Kuklo took Sharle and escaped from Wall Sheena.

In Shiganshina District, the Survey Corps was preparing for its first expedition outside of the wall in fifteen years. Kuklo wanted to see a Titan to confirm that he wasn't like them, that he was indeed a human being. He left Sharle behind and snuck into the expedition's cargo wagon. As he hoped, the Survey Corps ran across a Titan, but it was far worse of a monster than he expected. The group suffered grievous losses, but thanks to Captain Carlo and Kuklo's idea, they eventually retreated safely behind Wall Maria. Kuklo helped the Survey Corps survive, but inside the walls he was greeted by the Military Police, who wanted the "Titan's Son" on charges of murdering Dario. In prison, he met Cardina, a young man jailed over political squabbles. They hoped to escape to safety when exiled beyond the Wall, but found themselves surrounded by a pack of Titans. It was through the help of Jorge, former Survey Corps Captain and first human to defeat a Titan, that the two boys escaped with their lives. The equipment that Jorge used was the very "Device" that was the key to defeating the Titan those fifteen years ago.

Kuklo and Cardina escaped the notice of the MPs by hiding in the industrial city, where they found Sharle. It is there that the three youngsters learned the truth of the ill-fated Titan-capturing expedition fifteen years earlier, and swore to uphold the will of Angel, the inventor of the Device.

Before the fall Character Profiles

Kuklo

A fifteen-year-old boy born from a dead body packed into the vomit of a Titan, which earned him the moniker, "Son of a Titan." He is fascinated with the Device as a means to defeat the Titans. The protagonist of this story.

Sharle Inocencio

First daughter of the Inocencios, a rich merchant family within Wall Sheena. When she realized that Kuklo was a human, she taught him to speak and learn. Currently an apprentice craftsman under Xenophon in the industrial city.

Xavi Inocencio

Head of the Inocencio family and Sharle's brother. Member of the Military Police in Shiganshina District.

Cardina Baumeister

Kuklo's first friend in the outside world, and his companion in developing the Device.

Jorge Pikale

Training Corps instructor. A former Survey Corps captain who was hailed as a hero for defeating a Titan.

Carlo Pikale

Jorge's son and current captain of the Survey Corps. After they battled Titans together, he has great respect for Kuklo.

Xenophon Harkimo

Foreman at the industrial city. He took over development of the Device from its inventor, Angel.

Gloria Bernhart

Captain of the Military Police in Shiganshina District. A powerful MP officer with a cold, tactical mind.

WHERE ARE THOSE TITAN-WORSHIP-PERS?!!
WHICH WAY DID THEY GO?!
GAH!
DAMDAMDAM
YES, SIR!
YOU GO AND REPORT TO CAPTAIN BERN-HART!
THERE'S AN INTERSEC-TION AHEAD! SPLIT INTO THREE GROUPS!
DID WE LOSE THEM ?!
CREEAK
STOMP STOMP STOMP
YES, SIR!!
AND CALL FOR BACKUP !!!

Based on "Attack on Titan"
created by Hajime Isayama
Story by: Ryo Suzukaze
Art by Satoshi Shiki
Character Designs by: Thores Shibamoto

Contents:

Chapter 21: Den of Treachery... 1
Chapter 22: Abyss Below the Wall... 61
Chapter 23: Rondo of Darkness... 113
Chapter 24: Wail from the Shadows... 165
Swear Upon Wall Maria... 217

ATTACK ON TITAN
7
BEFORE THE FALL

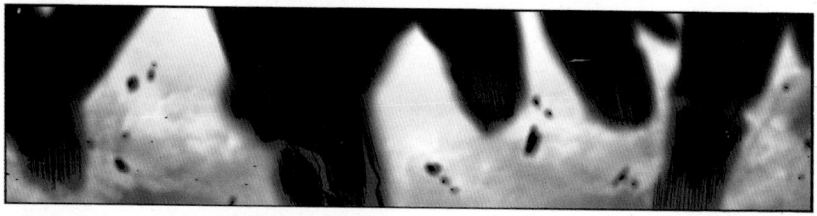